COLLINS GEM

ANTIQUE MARKS

Anna Selby
and
The Diagram Group

HarperCollins*Publishers*

HarperCollins Publishers
PO Box, Glasgow G4 0NB

A Diagram book first created by Diagram Visual Information Limited of 195 Kentish Town Road, London NW5 8SY

First published 1994
This edition published 1999

Reprint 10 9 8 7 6 5 4 3 2 1 0

ISBN 0 00 472286-8

Printed in Italy by Amadeus S.p.A.

Introduction

Do you ever attend car boot sales or browse in antique shops in search of bargains? Have you ever wished you knew more about grandma's silver spoon or that old piece of china which has been around your home for so many years? Do you envy the experts' ability to identify and date such fascinating hand-me-downs? If the answer to any of these questions is yes, then *Collins Gem Antique Marks* is for you.

This handy reference work offers a wealth of detailed information which you can refer to at home, yet in a format which is small enough to slip into your bag or pocket. It can always be right at hand, ready to help you seize the chance of 'a good buy', or perhaps to protect you against an unwise purchase.

The book begins with a clear and thorough guide to the hallmarks stamped on British silver and gold ever since the Middle Ages, and those now found on platinum. There follows coverage of the quite different marks to be found on Old Sheffield Plate. A representative selection of Pewter makers' marks is provided next, as an introduction to these once so common household wares. Lastly, the book surveys the vast range of marks to be found on pottery and porcelain, both from Britain and the rest of Europe, and from China and Japan.

While the depth of knowledge of the true expert requires years of experience in handling and studying antiques, *Collins Gem Antique Marks* will provide you with the instant means to interpret the marks which are so often crucial in assessing antique objects.

Contents

1. Hallmarks on silver, gold and platinum

Silver and gold have long been prized for their useful and attractive properties. Gold was one of the first metals to be discovered. Being soft and easy to work, colourful, bright and resistant to corrosion, it was ideal for jewellery and other decorative objects. Its scarcity ensured that its value remained high. Silver is harder and less scarce than gold, and thus more widely used in everyday life. Both silver and gold have been mined in Britain since Roman times, in modest quantities. Platinum was unknown in Europe until 1600, only became available commercially in the 19th century, and has only been regulated in Britain since 1975. Used mainly for jewellery, it is more precious than gold. The high value of these three metals makes it essential to have legally enforced standards of purity. The craft of the silversmith has been regulated by Parliamentary Acts and Royal Ordinances since the late 12th century. Since 1 January 1975, a simplified scheme of hallmarks has been in use for British silver, gold and platinum, as directed by the Hallmarking Act of 1973.

PRE-1975 HALLMARKS AND WHAT THEY MEAN

Under the British regulations, any object made of silver or gold is stamped with various ‘hallmarks’ which enable us to tell when it was made, by whom, where it was manufactured or tested for purity, and, most important of all, how pure it is. The term 'hallmark' is derived from Goldsmiths' Hall, the guild hall of the London Goldsmiths' Company, the body which oversaw the first assay marks in Britain. In 1300, the Sterling standard was established at 925 parts of silver per 1000 in an object, just as in English coinage. No object was allowed to leave the craftsman's hands until it had been assayed (tested) and marked with a punch depicting a leopard's head, a mark which is still used on London silver. Other assay offices were established in the English provinces, and in Scotland and Ireland, and all but the smallest had their own mark of origin.

From 1363, each craftsman was required to add his own 'maker's mark' and to register it.

From 1478, a 'date mark' was required to be struck, consisting of a letter of the alphabet which signified the year in which the piece had been assayed. This made it possible to trace the 'Keeper of the Touch' who had assayed a particular piece, in case of later disputes as to purity. It now allows us to determine an accurate date for any piece of British plate.

A 'duty mark' depicting the head of the current monarch is found on plate assayed between 1784 and 1890, as proof that a tax on silver goods had been paid by the maker. The duty mark should not be confused with later commemorative stamps which mark special occasions such as Coronations and Jubilees.

Marks of origin on British silver to 1974

The mark of origin, or assay office mark, identifies the town or city where the item in question was assayed, and probably manufactured. Since 1300, London has used the leopard's head (**1**) (sometimes crowned, sometimes not). An exception is the period 1697–1720 when the 'lion's head erased' (**2**) was used, when the Britannia standard replaced the Sterling standard for English silver. At Edinburgh, the earliest Scottish assay office, the mark of origin has always been a three-towered castle (**3**). Dublin has used a harp crowned (**4**) since the mid 17th century. As further examples, Birmingham has long used an anchor (**5**), and Sheffield used a crown (**6**) for many years. More specific information on marks of origin will be found in the introductions to the tables of each city's hallmarks, later in the present chapter.

Sample marks of origin

1 2 3 4 5 6

Makers' marks

Since 1363, silversmiths have been required to stamp their work with a registered mark. Thus one can identify the maker of a particular piece – at least if it was made after about 1666, when the earlier registers at Goldsmiths' Hall were burnt in the Great Fire of London. At first the custom was to use a rebus (for example a picture of a fox for a silversmith whose surname was Fox) and initials combined in one mark. From 1697, makers were required by law to use the first two letters of their surnames (**a**, **b**), but from 1720 initials again became the norm (**c**, **d**), sometimes with a symbol added (**e**, **f**).

In Scotland before about 1700, makers commonly used a monogram (**g**, **h**), but this died out to be replaced by plain initials (**i**). Some used their full surname (**j**). In the case of factories or firms (**k**), the maker's mark is often called the 'sponsor's mark'.

Sample makers' marks

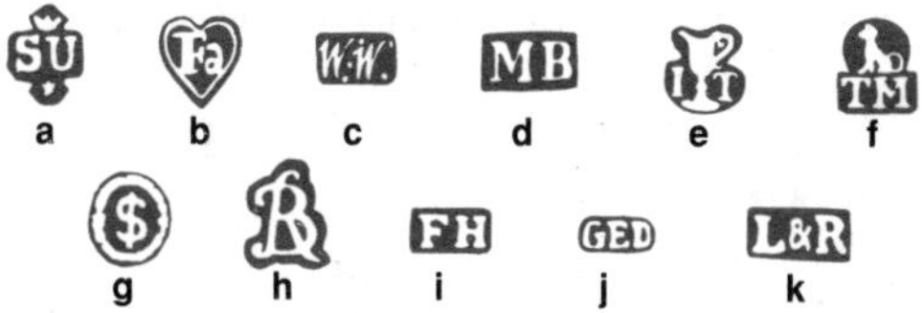

a Thomas Sutton, London 1711
b John Farnell, London 1714
c William Woodward, London 1741
d Mathew Boulton, Birmingham 1790
e John Tuite, London 1739
f Thomas Morse, London 1720
g James Sympsone, Edinburgh 1687
h Robert Brook, Glasgow 1673
i Francis Howden, Edinburgh 1781
j Dougal Ged, Edinburgh 1734
k Lothian and Robertson, Edinburgh 1746

Date letters to 1974

Date letters were introduced in England from 1478, in Scotland (Edinburgh) from 1681, and in Ireland (Dublin) from 1638. The date letter system means that every item of hallmarked silver (and gold) carries a stamp indicating the year when it was assayed. The date stamp takes the form of a letter of the alphabet, changed to the next letter annually in a regular cycle, rather like present-day car registrations. Different assay offices have used different cycles, omitting various letters of the alphabet to form sequences lasting from 19 to 26 years. 'I' was often used for 'J'. Each new cycle was given a new style of lettering and shape of shield, so as to distinguish one cycle from another. The exact day of the year when the letter was changed varied at the different assay offices, and so is given in the introduction to each town later in this chapter.

Sample date letters

1 2 3 4 5 6

1 London 1561
2 London 1936
3 Birmingham 1891
4 Chester 1742
5 Dublin 1662
6 Edinburgh 1968

Standard marks to 1974

In England before 1544, the Sterling silver standard of 92.5% purity (925 parts per 1000) was vouched for by the leopard's head mark of the London Assay Office (**a**). In 1544, Henry VIII debased the coinage to only one third silver, and so a specific 'standard mark' showing a lion passant (**b**) was introduced, to be marked on items which met the Sterling standard. In 1697, the Sterling standard was replaced by the Britannia standard of 95.84% purity (958.4 parts per 1000), to stop the melting down of coins for plate. The Britannia figure (**c**) now replaced the lion passant as the standard mark, and the lion's head erased (**d**) replaced the leopard's head as the mark of origin. From 1720, the Sterling standard and its lion passant mark were reintroduced, but silver of the higher standard (although less common) continued to be marked with Britannia and the lion's head erased right up to 1974. Edinburgh and Glasgow used different standards of fineness (as described on page 38) until 1836, when they adopted the Sterling and Britannia standards.

Sample standard marks

a **b** **c** **d**

Duty marks 1784–1890

Between 1784 and 1890 a duty (tax) was imposed on silver in Britain. To prove that the duty had been paid by the silversmith, an extra mark depicting the head of the current king or queen was struck on most items of silverware produced in England in those years. (In Dublin the duty was imposed only from 1807 and in Glasgow from 1819.) Silversmiths had many tricks to avoid paying duty, so the mark is not always present.

Duty marks

1 **2** **3** **4**

1 George III (1760–1820)
2 George IV (1820–1830)
3 William IV (1830–1837)
4 Victoria (1837–1901)

Commemorative marks

Special marks have been added in certain calendar years to mark notable occasions. A mark with the heads of both King George V and Queen Mary (**1**) was used to mark their Silver Jubilee in 1935. The Coronation of Elizabeth II in 1953 was commemorated with a mark of the Queen's head (**2**). A similar mark (**3**) was used again to mark her Jubilee in 1977. Special commemorative marks have also been used by the Dublin, Birmingham and Sheffield assay offices to celebrate various anniversaries in the 1970s and 1980s. Because of the exact time of year when the date letter was changed at a particular assay office, such marks may appear not only with the date letter of the year commemorated, but also with that of the year before or the one after.

1

2

3

Marks on foreign silver to 1974

From 1867, a letter F (**a**) was stamped on foreign plate imported into Britain. From 1904, the decimal value of the Sterling (**b**) and Britannia (**c**) standards was marked on imported silver which met those standards, and each assay office had a special mark of origin, as used on imported gold (see page 136), but in an oval shield.

a

b

c

THE HALLMARKING ACT OF 1973

In 1973 a new Act of Parliament was passed for regulating and simplifying the law regarding hallmarks on silver, gold and platinum in Britain, and it came into force on 1 January 1975. The Act governs hallmarks at the four remaining assay offices, in London, Edinburgh, Birmingham and Sheffield (but not Dublin, which since 1921 has been the captial of the independent Irish Republic). All items weighing more than 7.8 grams must be hallmarked before they can be described as silver (for gold it is any item above 1 gram, and for platinum above 0.5 gram). There are four hallmarks in total: the registered maker's or sponsor's mark, the standard mark, the mark of origin (assay office mark), and the date letter.

Sample modern silver hallmarks

1 2 3 4

1 Maker's mark **2** Standard mark
3 Mark of origin **4** Date letter

Standard marks from 1975

On Sterling silver, the London, Birmingham and Sheffield Assay Offices still use the traditional lion passant (**a**), while Edinburgh uses the lion rampant (**b**). At all four offices, the Britannia mark (**c**) is used (without the old accompanying lion's head erased) on silver which meets the Britannia standard.

 a  b  c

Marks of Origin from 1975

Only four assay offices remained open in Britain by 1975. London still uses a leopard's head (**1**). Birmingham still uses its anchor (**2**) and Edinburgh its three-towered castle (**3**). However, Sheffield has adopted a York rose (**4**) to replace the crown which it had used for over 200 years, because the crown risked being confused with a similar mark on gold. Dublin is not affected by the Act, and still uses its harp crowned.

1 2 3 4

Date letters from 1975

The date letter now coincides exactly with the calendar year, it being changed on 1 January every year, and the same style is used by all four British assay offices.

Imported foreign silver from 1975

The marking of imported foreign silver has been simplified and standardized under the 1973 Act. The standard mark consists of the millesimal value in an oval shield (see below). The marks of origin used by the four assay offices are similar to those on foreign gold and platinum, but in an oval shield (see below).

Sterling Britannia

London Birmingham Sheffield Edinburgh

Convention marks

In the past, UK makers had difficulty exporting British silver and gold, because the hallmarks were not legally recognised abroad. Importers faced similar problems. Therefore the European Free Trade Association has produced a convention on the control and marking of precious metals, and the UK has been a signatory since 1976. Under this arrangement, a set of 'convention marks' is commonly recognized. They consist of a common control mark (see below) giving the standard of fineness, the fineness again in numerals, also a mark of origin and a sponsor's (maker's) mark. These marks are struck in place of, or in addition to, the usual British or foreign marks. The system of convention marks means that precious metals assayed in countries which are signatories can be imported and exported between those countries without being re-assayed.

Control marks

	Gold	18 carat
	Gold	14 carat
	Gold	9 carat
	Silver	Sterling
	Platinum	

Note that in the UK, any silver below Sterling (925) standard is not approved. Britannia silver and 22 carat gold are not recognized under the convention.

The British Hallmarking Council

A body called the British Hallmarking Council was established under the 1973 Act, and became operative in 1975. The Council coordinates the activities of the four assay offices, without hindering their independence. Its main responsibility is to ensure that adequate assaying facilities are available in the UK, and to see that laws relating to assaying are adhered to.

READING THE HALLMARK CHARTS IN THIS BOOK

Layout of the hallmark charts

The charts on the pages which follow show the hallmarks associated with each of the towns or cities which have had important assay offices, presented in the order in which the assay offices were established. Within each section, all the variations in the design of that city's mark of origin (**b**) and the standard marks (**c** and sometimes **d**) are illustrated, and these are followed by any duty marks or commemorative marks (**e**) and by the date letters (**f**). Unusual marks are fully explained in special feature panels (**a**). Makers' marks are shown separately in lists at the end of each city's section.
For gold, the marks of origin are the same as for silver, except in the cases of Birmingham and Dublin (see pages 134–135). Date letters are the same for gold and platinum as they are for silver.
Note that the hallmark charts apply primarily to silver (as they show the standard marks for silver), but that the same date letters apply equally to British gold.

Here is a sample of a set of marks which you may be looking for (although they may not appear in this order):

a
SP
b
c
e
f
h

In the charts they would be shown as follows:

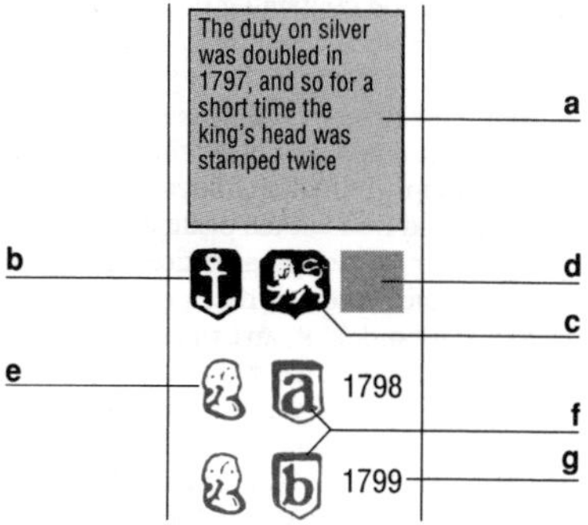
The duty on silver was doubled in 1797, and so for a short time the king's head was stamped twice
a
b
d
c
e
a
1798
f
g
b
1799

a Text box for unusual markings
b Mark of origin
c Standard mark
d Possible second standard mark
e Duty or commemorative mark
f Date letter mark
g Text showing year
h Maker's mark (see lists of makers' marks following each city's hallmark charts)

HOW TO READ HALLMARKS

When looking at hallmarks, begin by studying the mark of origin, to find out where the piece was assayed. (If no assay office's mark is present, the piece probably comes from London.) Then turn to the relevant city's section in the tables of hallmarks. Now look at the date letter. This is probably the hardest part of the process. Examine the letter to see whether it is a capital or a small letter, check what kind of script it is in, and note the shape of the shield containing it. Compare these features with the letters in the correct city's tables. Only when you find the example in the table which exactly matches your hallmark can you be confident about its date. Once the place and date of origin are established, it is relatively simple to look up the maker's or sponsor's mark and find out the name of the craftsman or company. Other marks will give extra information, such as whether the piece is Sterling or Britannia silver, whether duty was paid on it, and whether it was made in a Coronation or Jubilee year.

LONDON

The Goldsmiths' Company in London was the first in England authorized to assay and mark gold and silver, after the granting of a Royal Charter in 1327. London has been by far the most important British assay office, both in terms of the high quality of workmanship it maintained, and of the amount and variety of silverware passing through it.

London's mark of origin is a leopard's head, crowned from 1478 to 1821 and thereafter uncrowned. The shape of the head and crown have varied over the years, as has the shield surrounding them. From 1697 until 1720 (while the Britannia standard was in force) the leopard's head was replaced by the lion's head erased and the Britannia mark. From 1784 to 1890, the sovereign's head duty mark was in use.

From 1478 to 1974, London traditionally used a 20-letter sequence (A to U omitting J), with the letter being changed in May each year. Since 1975 all British date letter sequences have been standardized, and are changed on 1 January. In the same year platinum was first assayed and marked here.

The London Assay Office is still in operation.

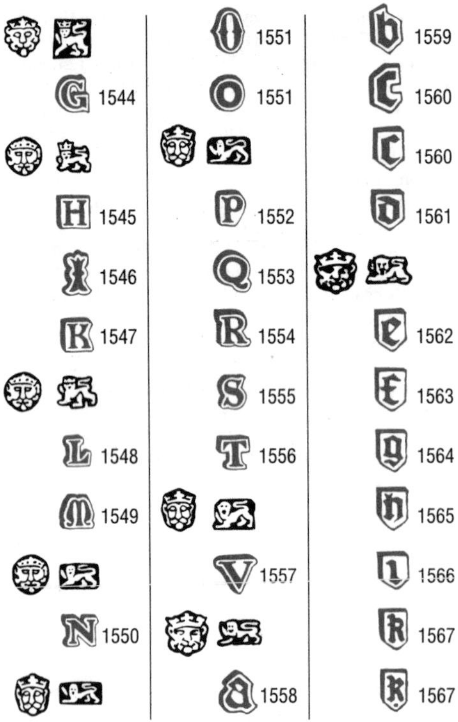

1544
1545
1546
1547
1548
1549
1550
1551
1551
1552
1553
1554
1555
1556
1557
1558
1559
1560
1560
1561
1562
1563
1564
1565
1566
1567
1567

l 1568
m 1569
n 1570
o 1571
p 1572
q 1573
r 1574
s (with cross) 1575
s 1575
t 1576
u 1577

A 1578
B 1579
C 1580
D 1581
E 1582
F 1583
G 1584
H 1585
I 1586
K 1587
L 1588
M 1589

N 1590
O 1591

P 1592
Q 1593
R 1594
S 1595
T 1596
V 1597

A 1598
B 1599

C	1600	P	1612	f	1623
D	1601	Q	1613	g	1624
E	1602	R	1614	h	1625
F	1603	S	1615	i	1626
G	1604	T	1616	k	1627
H	1605	V	1617	l	1628
I	1606			m	1629
K	1607	a	1618	n	1630
L	1608	b	1619	o	1631
M	1609	c	1620	p	1632
N	1610	d	1621	q	1633
O	1611	e	1622	r	1634

 1635

 1636

 1637

 1638

 1639

 1640

 1641

 1642

 1643

 1644

 1645

 1646

 1647

 1648

 1649

 1650

 1651

 1652

 1653

 1654

 1655

 1656

 1657

 1658

 1659

 1660

 1661

 1662

 1663

 1664

 1665

 1666

 1667

 1668

 1669

 1670

 1671

 1672

 1672

 1673

 1674

 1675

 1676

 1677

 1678

 1679

 1680

 1681

 1682

 1683

 1684

 1685

 1686

 1687

 1688

 1689

 1690

 1691

 1692

 1693

 1694

 1695

 1696 1697

 1697

 1697

1698

1699

1700

1701

1702

1702

1703

1704

1705

1706

1707

1708

1709

1710

1711

1712

1713

1714

1715

1716

1717

1718

1719

1720

1721

1722

1723

1724

1725

1726

M 1727

N 1728

From 1716 to 1728, the shield shape for the date letter occasionally varied

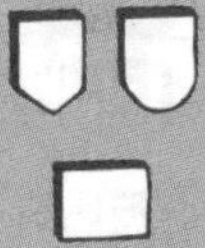

O 1729

P 1730

Q 1731

R 1732

S 1733

T 1734

V 1735

a 1736

b 1737

c 1738

d 1739

d 1739

e 1740

f 1741

g 1742

h 1743

i 1744

k 1745

l 1746

m 1747

n 1748

o 1749

p 1750

q 1751

r 1752

ſ 1753

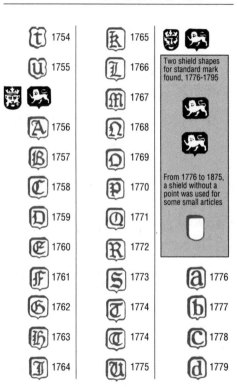

t 1754

u 1755

A 1756

B 1757

C 1758

D 1759

E 1760

F 1761

G 1762

H 1763

I 1764

k 1765

L 1766

M 1767

N 1768

O 1769

P 1770

Q 1771

R 1772

S 1773

T 1774

T 1774

U 1775

Two shield shapes for standard mark found, 1776-1795

From 1776 to 1875, a shield without a point was used for some small articles

a 1776

b 1777

c 1778

d 1779

Letter	Year
e	1780
f	1781
g	1782
h	1783
i	1784
k	1785
l	1786
m	1787
n	1788
o	1789
p	1790
q	1791
r	1792
s	1793
t	1794
u	1795

Letter	Year
A	1796
B	1797
C	1798
D	1799
E	1800
F	1801
G	1802
H	1803
I	1804
K	1805
L	1806
M	1807
N	1808
O	1809
P	1810
Q	1811
R	1812
S	1813
T	1814

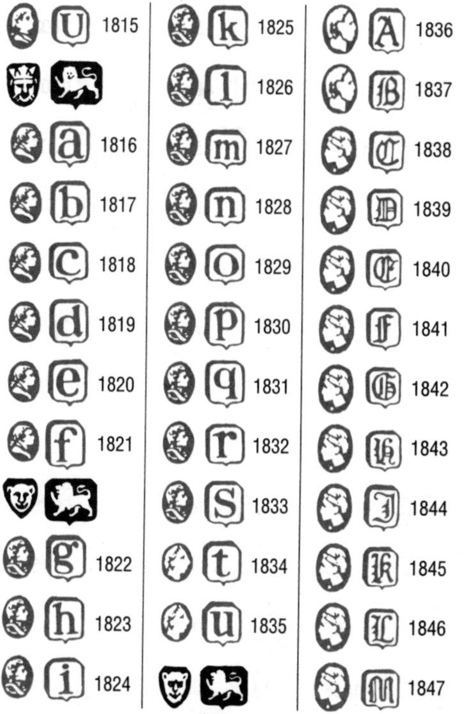
1815
1816
1817
1818
1819
1820
1821
1822
1823
1824
1825
1826
1827
1828
1829
1830
1831
1832
1833
1834
1835
1836
1837
1838
1839
1840
1841
1842
1843
1844
1845
1846
1847

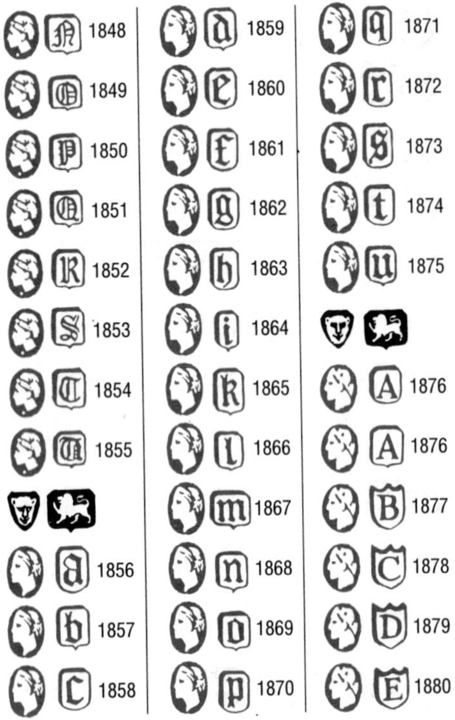
1848
1849
1850
1851
1852
1853
1854
1855
1856
1857
1858
1859
1860
1861
1862
1863
1864
1865
1866
1867
1868
1869
1870
1871
1872
1873
1874
1875
1876
1876
1877
1878
1879
1880

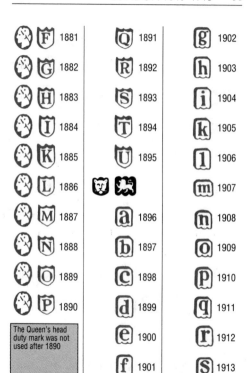

Date letter	Year
F	1881
G	1882
H	1883
I	1884
K	1885
L	1886
M	1887
N	1888
O	1889
P	1890

The Queen's head duty mark was not used after 1890

Date letter	Year
Q	1891
R	1892
S	1893
T	1894
U	1895

Date letter	Year
a	1896
b	1897
c	1898
d	1899
e	1900
f	1901
g	1902
h	1903
i	1904
k	1905
l	1906
m	1907
n	1908
o	1909
p	1910
q	1911
r	1912
s	1913

t 1914
u 1915

a 1916
b 1917
c 1918
d 1919
e 1920
f 1921
g 1922
h 1923
i 1924
k 1925
l 1926
m 1927
n 1928
o 1929
p 1930
q 1931
r 1932
s 1933

 t 1934
 u 1935

A 1936
B 1937
C 1938
D 1939
E 1940
F 1941
G 1942
H 1943
I 1944
K 1945
L 1946

M 1947

N 1948

O 1949

P 1950

Q 1951

 R 1952

 S 1953

T 1954

U 1955

a 1956

b 1957

c 1958

d 1959

e 1960

f 1961

g 1962

h 1963

i 1964

k 1965

l 1966

m 1967

n 1968

o 1969

p 1970

q 1971

r 1972

s 1973

t 1974

New letter sequence commenced on 1 January 1975, in accordance with the Hallmarking Act passed in 1973

A 1975

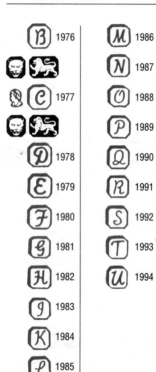

B 1976

 C 1977

D 1978

E 1979

F 1980

G 1981

H 1982

I 1983

K 1984

L 1985

M 1986

N 1987

O 1988

P 1989

Q 1990

R 1991

S 1992

T 1993

U 1994

LONDON MAKERS' MARKS

ABS	Adey B Savory
AF SG	Andrew Fogelberg & Stephen Gilbert
AS	Thomas Ash
BC	Benjamin Cooper
BS	Benjamin Smith
BS BS	Benjamin Smith & Son
Bu/BU	Thomas Burridge
CF	Charles Fox or Crispin Fuller
CK	Charles F Kandler (star below)
CO	Augustin Courtauld (fleur-de-lys above)
CR	Charles Rawlins
CR DR	Christian & David Reid
CR GS	Charles Reilly & George Storer
CR WS	Charles Rawlins & William Summers
DH	David Hennell
DM	Dorothy Mills
DPW	Dobson, Prior & Williams
DS BS	Digby Scott & Benjamin Smith
DS RS	Daniel Smith & Robert Sharp
EC	Ebenezer Coker
EF	Edward Feline
ET	Elizabeth Tuite
EW	Edward Wigan
EY	Edward Yorke
FC	Francis Crump
FO	Thomas Folkingham
GA	George Adams
GS	George Smith
GS WF	George Smith & William Fearn
GW	George Wintle
HA	Pierre Harache (crown above)
HB	Hester Bateman
HC	Henry Chawner
HC IE	Henry Chawner & John Emes
HN	Hannah Northcote
IB	James Bult
IC	John Carter
IG	John Gould
IH	John Hyatt
IL HL	John & Henry Lias
IL HL CL	John, Henry & Charles Lias
IP	John Pollock

LONDON MAKERS' MARKS (continued)

Mark	Maker
IS	John Swift or John Scholfield
IW IT	John Walcelon & John Taylor
JA	Joseph Angell
JA JA	J & J Aldous
JC	John Cafe
JE	John Emes
JL	John Lias
LA	Paul de Lamerie (crown and star above)
LO	Nathaniel Lock
LP	Lewis Pantin
MC	Mary Chawner
ME	Louis Mettayer
MP	Mary Pantin
MS	Mary Sumner
MS ES	Mary & Elizabeth Sumner
Ne	Anthony Nelme
NS	Nicholas Sprimont
PB AB	Peter & Anne Bateman
PB AB WB	Peter, Anne & William Bateman
PB IB	Peter & Jonathan Bateman
PL	Pierre Platel
PL	Paul de Lamerie (crown and star above, fleur-de-lys below)
PS	Paul Storr
Py	Benjamin Pyne (rose and crown above)
RC	Richard Crossley
RC GS	Richard Crossley & George Smith
R DH H	Robert & David Hennell
RE EB	Rebecca Emes & Edward Barnard
RE WE	Rebecca & William Emes
RG	Robert Garrard
RH	Robert Hennell
RH DH	Robert & David Hennell
RH DH SH	Robert, David & Samuel Hennell
RH SH	Robert & Samuel Hennell
RM RC	Robert Makepeace & Richard Carter

RM **TM**	Robert & Thomas Makepeace
Ro	Philip Rolles
RR	Richard Rugg or Robert Rutland
RS	Robert Swanson
SA	Stephen Adams
Sc	William Scarlett
SC **IC**	S & J Crespell
SG	Samuel Godbehere
SG **EW**	Samuel Godbehere & Edward Wigan
SL	Gabriel Sleath
SM	Samuel Meriton
Sp	Thomas Spackman
S **WI** **A**	Stephen Adams & William Jury
TH	Thomas Heming
TH **IC**	Thomas Hannam & John Crouch
T & W	Turner & Williams
TN	Thomas Northcote
TO	Thomas Oliphant
TP **ER**	Thomas Phipps & Edward Robinson
TP **ER** **JP**	Thomas Phipps, Edward Robinson & James Phipps
TP **IP**	Thomas & James Phipps

TR	Thomas Robins
T **WC** **C**	Thomas & William Chawner
WB	William Burwash
WC	William Cafe
WE	William Eaton or William Eley
WE **CE** **HE**	William, Charles & Henry Eley
WE **GP**	William Eley & George Pierrepont
WE **WF**	William Eley & William Fearn
WF	William Fearn
WF **PS**	William Frisbee & Paul Storr
WG	William Grundy
WI	David Willaume
WP	William Peaston or William Plummer
WRS	W R Smiley
WS	William Sumner or William Smiley
WT	William Tweedie
W **WP** **S**	William Shaw & William Priest

EDINBURGH

Silver was assayed in Edinburgh from the middle of the 15th century, although the first known specimens date from a century later than that. There was an Incorporation of Goldsmiths here from at least the 1490s. Over the years Edinburgh has been known particularly for ecclesiastical and domestic silverware.
The Edinburgh mark of origin is a three-towered castle.
Before 1681 the standard mark took the form of the Deacon's mark, a monogram of the initials of the current holder of that office. From 1681 the Deacon's mark was replaced by the Assay Master's mark, again consisting of the office-holder's initials. This was replaced in 1759 by a thistle, which changed in 1975 to a lion rampant. From 1784 to 1890 the sovereign's head duty mark was in use.

From 1457 to 1836, Edinburgh used a standard of 916.6 parts of silver per thousand, except in 1489–1555 when the Standard of Bruges was used (varying from 917 to 946 parts per thousand according to the size of the object). Only from 1836 was the Sterling standard adopted at Edinburgh.

Date letters came into use in 1681. Edinburgh generally used a 25-letter sequence, omitting J (although it was included in 1789 and 1815). The letter was changed in October. From 1 January 1975 the standard British date letter sequence has been used.

The Edinburgh Assay Office is still in operation. Platinum was first marked here in 1982.

Marks	Date
	1556
	1563
	1565
	1575
	1576
	1577
	1585
	1591
	1598
	1609
	1611
	1617
	circa 1617
	1613-1621
	1616-1635
	1637
	1640
	1642
	1643
	1644
	1649
	1651
	1660
	1665
	1669
	1663-1681
	1675

	1681

	1682
	1683
	1684
	1685
	1686
	1687

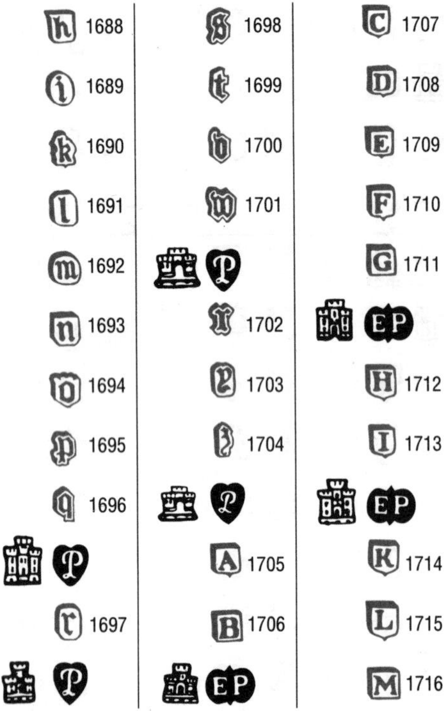
1688
1689
1690
1691
1692
1693
1694
1695
1696
1697
1698
1699
1700
1701
1702
1703
1704
1705
1706
1707
1708
1709
1710
1711
EP
1712
1713
EP
1714
1715
1716
EP

N 1717

EP

O 1718

P 1719

P 1719

EP

Q 1720

R 1721

S 1722

T 1723

U 1724

V 1725

V 1725

W 1726

X 1727

Y 1728

Z 1729

AU

A 1730

B 1731

C 1732

D 1733

E 1734

F 1735

G 1736

H 1737

I 1738

K 1739

GED

L 1740

M 1741

E·L

N 1742

O 1743

HG

P 1744

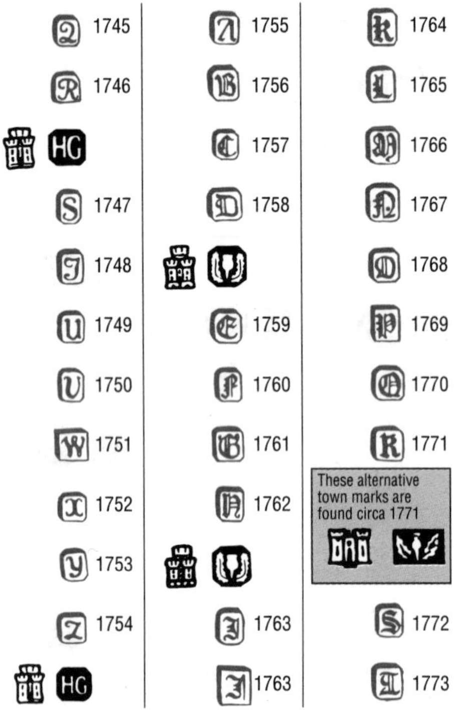

1745
1746
HG
1747
1748
1749
1750
1751
1752
1753
1754
HG

1755
1756
1757
1758
1759
1760
1761
1762
1763
1763

1764
1765
1766
1767
1768
1769
1770
1771

These alternative town marks are found circa 1771

1772
1773

1774
1775
1776
1777
1778
1779
A 1780
B 1781
C 1782
D 1783
E 1784
F 1785
G 1786-1787
H 1788
I 1789
J 1789
K 1790
L 1791
M 1792
N 1793
N 1793
O 1794
O 1794
P 1795
Q 1796
R 1797
R 1797
S 1798
T 1799
U 1800
V 1801
W 1802

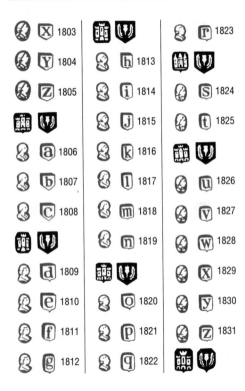

X 1803
Y 1804
Z 1805
a 1806
b 1807
c 1808
d 1809
e 1810
f 1811
g 1812

h 1813
i 1814
j 1815
k 1816
l 1817
m 1818
n 1819
o 1820
p 1821
q 1822

r 1823
s 1824
t 1825
u 1826
v 1827
w 1828
x 1829
y 1830
z 1831

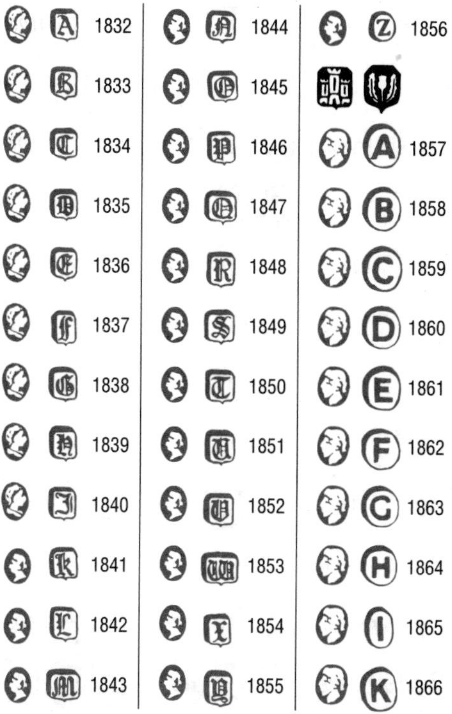
1832
1833
1834
1835
1836
1837
1838
1839
1840
1841
1842
1843
1844
1845
1846
1847
1848
1849
1850
1851
1852
1853
1854
1855
1856
1857
1858
1859
1860
1861
1862
1863
1864
1865
1866

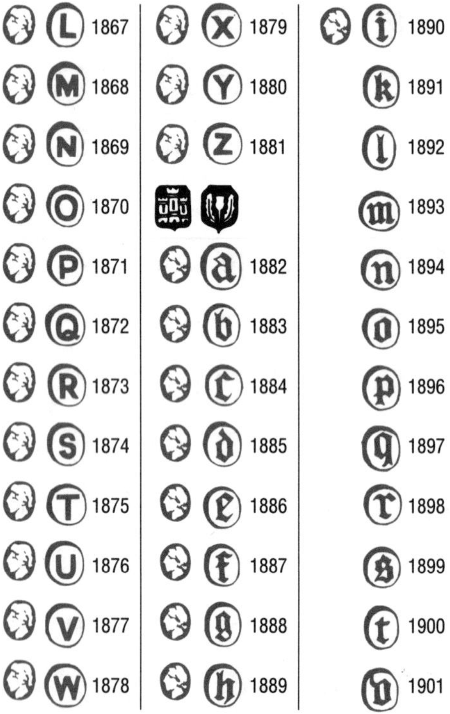
L 1867
M 1868
N 1869
O 1870
P 1871
Q 1872
R 1873
S 1874
T 1875
U 1876
V 1877
W 1878
X 1879
Y 1880
Z 1881
a 1882
b 1883
c 1884
d 1885
e 1886
f 1887
g 1888
h 1889
i 1890
k 1891
l 1892
m 1893
n 1894
o 1895
p 1896
q 1897
r 1898
s 1899
t 1900
u 1901

w	1902
r	1903
y	1904
z	1905

A	1906
B	1907
C	1908
D	1909
E	1910
F	1911
G	1912
H	1913
I	1914
K	1915
L	1916
M	1917
N	1918
O	1919
P	1920
Q	1921
R	1922
S	1923
T	1924
U	1925
V	1926
W	1927
X	1928
Y	1929
Z	1930

A	1931
B	1932
C	1933

D	1934

E 1935

F 1936

G 1937

H 1938

I 1939

K 1940

L 1941

M 1942

N 1943

O 1944

P 1945

Q 1946

R 1947

S 1948

T 1949

U 1950

V 1951

W 1952

X 1953

Y 1954

Z 1955

A 1956

B 1957

C 1958

D 1959

E 1960

F 1961

G 1962

H 1963

I 1964

k 1965

Letter	Year
L	1966
M	1967
N	1968
O	1969
P	1970
Q	1971
R	1972
S	1973-1974

New letter sequence commenced from 1 January 1975, following the Hallmarking Act passed in 1973

Letter	Year
A	1975
B	1976

Letter	Year
C	1977

Letter	Year
D	1978
E	1979
F	1980
G	1981
H	1982
I	1983
K	1984
L	1985
M	1986
N	1987
O	1988
P	1989
Q	1990
R	1991
S	1992
T	1993
U	1994

EDINBURGH MAKERS' MARKS

AE	Alexander Edmonstone
AG	Alexander Gairdner
AH	Alexander Henderson
AK	Alexander Kincaid
AS	Alexander Spencer
AZ	Alexander Zeigler
CD	Charles Dixon
E&Co	Elder & Co
EL	Edward Lothian
EO	Edward Oliphant
GC	George Christie
GF	George Fenwick
G&K	Gilsland & Ker
GMH	George McHattie
GS	George Scott
HB	Henry Beathume
HG	Hugh Gordon
ID	James Dempster
IG	John Gilsland
IK	James Ker
IR	James Rollo
IW	John Walsh
IZ	John Zeigler
JD	James Douglas
JM	Jonathan Millidge
JMc	John McKay
JN	James Nasmyth
J&WM	James & William Marshall
LO	Lawrence Oliphant
LU	Leonard Urquhart
MC	Matthew Craw
M & C	McKay & Chisholm
M & F	McKay & Fenwick
M & S	Marshall & Sons
MY	Mungo Yorstoun
PM	Peter Mathie
PR	Patrick Robertson
PS	Peter Sutherland
RB	Robert Bowman
RC	Robert Clark
RG	Robert Gordon
RI	Robert Inglis
RK	Robert Ker
WG	William Ged
W & PC	William & Peter Cunningham
WR	William Robertson
WS	Walter Scott
WT IT	William & Jonathan Taylor

YORK

The assaying of silver in York dates from the mid 16th century. York silver generally followed Scandinavian styles, and is known for pieces of basic design intended for everyday use. From 1717 to 1776 the York Assay Office was closed, and silver made there was assayed at Newcastle.

The York mark of origin was initially a halved leopard's head conjoined with a halved fleur-de-lys in a round shield. In the late 17th century the halved leopard's head was replaced by a halved seeded rose. This mark underwent numerous changes before, in 1701, it was replaced by a new mark depicting five lions passant on a cross, based on the York City coat of arms. From 1700 to 1850 a leopard's head accompanied the lion passant standard mark on York Sterling silver, while the Britannia mark and lion's head erased were used on York Britannia silver. From 1784 to 1856 (when the York Assay Office closed down), the sovereign's head duty mark was in use.

From at least 1607, York generally used a 24-letter date sequence omitting J and U, then from 1787 a 25-letter sequence omitting just J.

Mark	Date
	circa 1568
	circa 1577
	circa 1583
	circa 1594

Numerous versions of the town mark (see above) were used at the York Assay Office from c1560 to c1606

Mark	Date
F	1564
G	1565
H	1566
K	1568
L	1569
M	1570
O	1572
P	1573
Q	1574
R	1575
S	1576
T	1577
Z	1582
a	1583
b	1584
e	1587
h	1590
k	1592
l	1593
m	1594
n	1595
o	1596
p	1597
q	1598
r	1599
t	1601
x	1604
	circa 1608
	circa 1624

From 1607 to 1630, two versions of the town mark (see previous page) were used at the York Assay Office

 1607

 1608

 1609

 1610

 1611

 1612

 1613

 1614

 1615

 1616

 1617

 1618

 1619

 1620

 1621

 1622

 1623

 1624

 1625

 1626

 1627

 1628

 1629

 1630

From 1631 to 1656, two versions of the town mark (see below) were used at York Assay Office

 1631

 1632

 1633

 1634

 1635

f 1636
g 1637
h 1638
i 1639
k 1641
l 1642
m 1643
o 1645
s 1649
t 1650
u 1651
v 1652

w 1653
x 1654
y 1655
z 1656

A 1657
B 1658
C 1659
D 1660
E 1661
F 1662
G 1663

H 1664
I 1665
K 1666
L 1667
M 1668
N 1669
O 1670
P 1671
Q 1672
R 1673
S 1674
T 1675

1676
1677
1678
1679
1680
1681

From 1682 to 1699, two versions of the town mark (see below) were used at York Assay Office

circa 1680
circa 1696

1682
1683

1684
1685
1686
1687
1688
1689
1690
1691
1692
1693
1694
1695

1696
1697
1698
1699

1700
1701
1702
1703
1705
1706
1708

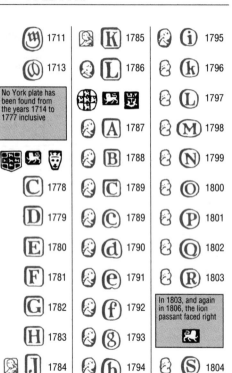

- 1711
- 1713

No York plate has been found from the years 1714 to 1777 inclusive

- C 1778
- D 1779
- E 1780
- F 1781
- G 1782
- H 1783
- J 1784

- K 1785
- L 1786

- A 1787
- B 1788
- C 1789
- c 1789
- d 1790
- e 1791
- f 1792
- g 1793
- h 1794

- i 1795
- k 1796
- l 1797
- M 1798
- N 1799
- O 1800
- P 1801
- Q 1802
- R 1803

In 1803, and again in 1806, the lion passant faced right

- S 1804

T	1805
U	1806
V	1807
W	1808
X	1809
Y	1810
Z	1811

a	1812
b	1813
c	1814
d	1815
e	1816
f	1817
g	1818
h	1819
i	1820
k	1821
l	1822
m	1823
n	1824
o	1825
p	1826
q	1827
r	1828
s	1829
t	1830
u	1831
v	1832
w	1833
x	1834
y	1835
z	1836

A	1837
B	1838

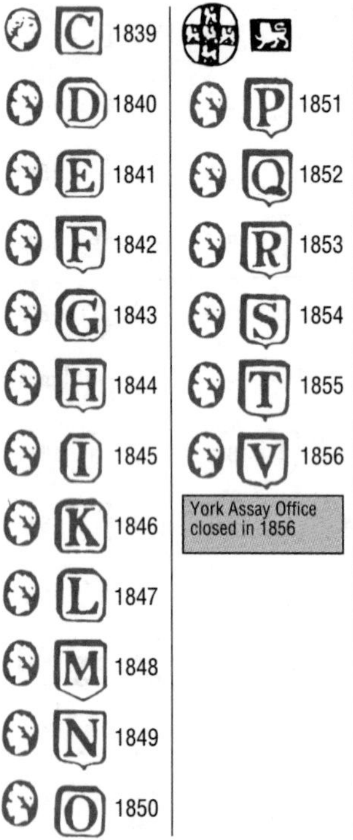
C 1839
D 1840
E 1841
F 1842
G 1843
H 1844
I 1845
K 1846
L 1847
M 1848
N 1849
O 1850
P 1851
Q 1852
R 1853
S 1854
T 1855
V 1856

York Assay Office closed in 1856

YORK MAKERS' MARKS

Mark	Maker(s)
BC &N	James Barber, George Cattle, William North
B & N	James Barber, William North
Bu	William Busfield
HP & C	John Hampston, John Prince, Robert Cattle
IH IP	John Hampston & John Prince
JB & Co	James Barber & Co
JB GC WN	James Barber, George Cattle, William North
JB WN	James Barber, William North
JB WW	James Barber, William Whitwell
La	John Langwith
Ma	Thomas Mangy
P & Co	John Prince, Robert Cattle
RC JB	Robert Cattle, James Barber

NORWICH

The earliest known Norwich silver marks date from the mid 16th century. The city is known principally for ecclesiastical and corporation plate.

The town mark was a lion passant surmounted by a castle. From the early 17th century another town mark was also in use, namely a seeded rose crowned, and variations of both marks appeared until 1701. After 1701, virtually no silver was assayed in Norwich.

Norwich used a 20-letter date sequence (A to V omitting J). The letter was changed each September.

There are no recorded makers' marks from Norwich.

A	1565
B	1566
C	1567
D	1568
E	1569
F	1570
G	1571
I	1573
K	1574
P	1579
	circa 1590
	circa 1595

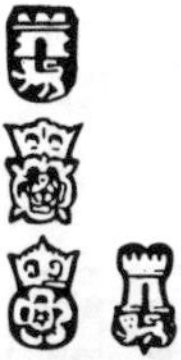

circa 1600

circa 1610

circa 1620

Several versions of the town marks shown below were used in 1624–1643 (e.g. as above for circa 1620)

A	1624
B	1625
C	1626
D	1627
E	1628
F	1629

G	1630
H	1631
I	1632
K	1633
L	1634
M	1635
N	1636
O	1637
P	1638
Q	1639
R	1640
S	1641

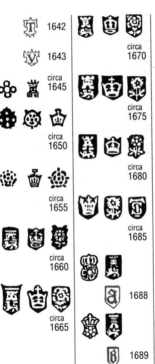

1642

1643

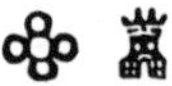
circa 1645

circa 1650

circa 1655

circa 1660

circa 1665

circa 1670

circa 1675

circa 1680

circa 1685

1688

1689

1691

1696

1697

1701

Little, if any, silver was assayed at Norwich after 1701

EXETER

The earliest assay marks date from the mid 16th century. Exeter is known for a good standard of ecclesiastical and domestic silver, but small items were rarely made.

The mark of origin was a round shield containing the letter X surmounted by a crown. After 1701, this was replaced with a three-towered castle. From 1701 to 1720, the Britannia mark and the lion's head erased were in use together as standard marks. After 1721, these were replaced with the leopard's head (omitted from 1777) and the lion passant in square shields. The sovereign's head duty mark was in use from 1784 to 1882.

The date letters began in 1701. Exeter initially used a 24-letter sequence (omitting J and U) then from 1797 a 20-letter sequnce (A to U omitting J). The date letter was changed in August.

Little silver was assayed in Exeter by the end of the 18th century, and the office closed in 1883.

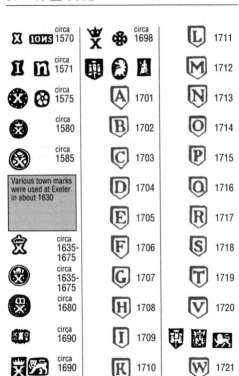

 circa 1570

 circa 1571

 circa 1575

 circa 1580

 circa 1585

Various town marks were used at Exeter in about 1630

 circa 1635-1675

 circa 1635-1675

 circa 1680

 circa 1690

 circa 1690

 circa 1698

 1701

 1702

 1703

 1704

 1705

 1706

 1707

 1708

 1709

 1710

 1711

 1712

 1713

 1714

 1715

 1716

 1717

 1718

 1719

 1720

 1721

X	1722
Y	1723
Z	1724

a	1725
b	1726
c	1727
d	1728
e	1729
f	1730
g	1731
h	1732
i	1733
k	1734
l	1735
m	1736
n	1737
o	1738
p	1739
q	1740
r	1741
s	1742
t	1743
u	1744
w	1745
x	1746
y	1747
z	1748

A	1749
B	1750
C	1751
D	1752
E	1753
F	1754
G	1755

H 1756
I 1757
K 1758
L 1759
M 1760
N 1761
O 1762
P 1763
Q 1764
R 1765
S 1766
T 1767

U 1768
W 1769
X 1770
Y 1771
Z 1772

A 1773
B 1774
C 1775
D 1776
E 1777

F 1778
G 1779
H 1780
I 1781-1782
K 1783

L 1784
M 1785
N 1786
O 1787
P 1788
q 1789
r 1790

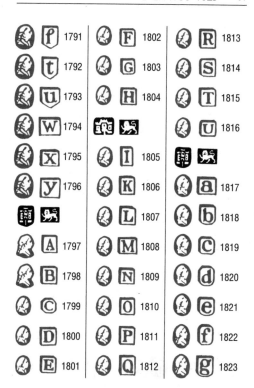

Date letter	Year
f	1791
t	1792
u	1793
W	1794
X	1795
y	1796
A	1797
B	1798
C	1799
D	1800
E	1801
F	1802
G	1803
H	1804
I	1805
K	1806
L	1807
M	1808
N	1809
O	1810
P	1811
Q	1812
R	1813
S	1814
T	1815
U	1816
a	1817
b	1818
c	1819
d	1820
e	1821
f	1822
g	1823

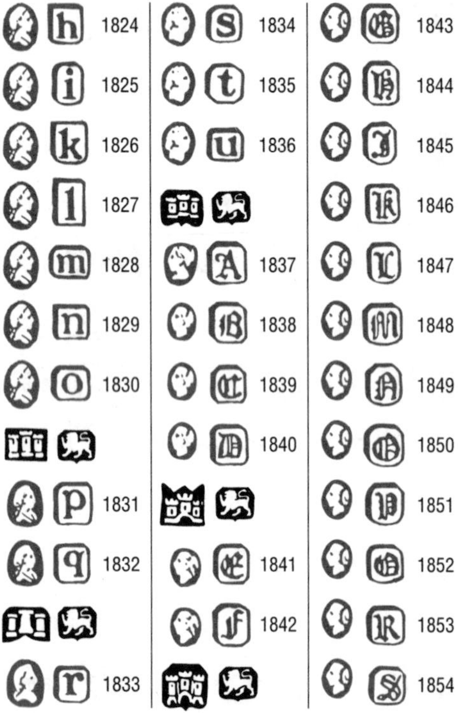
1824
1825
1826
1827
1828
1829
1830
1831
1832
1833
1834
1835
1836
1837
1838
1839
1840
1841
1842
1843
1844
1845
1846
1847
1848
1849
1850
1851
1852
1853
1854

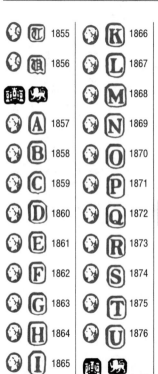

Date letter	Year
T	1855
U	1856
A	1857
B	1858
C	1859
D	1860
E	1861
F	1862
G	1863
H	1864
I	1865
K	1866
L	1867
M	1868
N	1869
O	1870
P	1871
Q	1872
R	1873
S	1874
T	1875
U	1876
A	1877
B	1878
C	1879
D	1880
E	1881
F	1882

Exeter Assay Office closed in 1883

EXETER MAKERS' MARKS

AR	Peter Arno	**RF**	Richard Ferris
DC	Daniel Coleman	**Ri**	Edward Richards
EI	John Elston	**RS**	Richard Sams
FR	Richard Freeman	**SB**	Samuel Blachford
GF	George Ferris	**SL**	Simon Lery
GT	George Turner	**Sy**	Pentycost Symonds
IB	John Buck	**TB**	Thomas Blake
IE	John Elston	**TE**	Thomas Eustace
IP	Isaac Parkin	**TR**	George Trowbridge
IW	John Williams	**TS**	Thomas Sampson
JH	Joseph Hicks	**Wi**	Richard Wilcocks
JO	John Osmont	**WP**	William Parry or William Pearse or William Pope
JS	John Stone or James Strong	**WRS**	W R Sobey
JW	James Williams	**WW**	William West
JW & Co	James Whipple & Co		
Mo	John Mortimer		

DUBLIN

Dublin's Goldsmiths' Company was given its charter in 1638, although silver had been made there long before and the Sterling standard was adopted as early as 1606. Dublin silver is known for a high standard of decorative workmanship.

The mark of origin is a harp crowned. Originally it also doubled as the standard mark. Up to 1719, two different versions of the harp crowned may be found, as shown in the tables. From 1731 the figure of Hibernia was added to show that duty had been paid. However, from 1807 when the sovereign's head mark was adopted as a duty mark (up to 1890, as in England), Hibernia was kept, and in time became regarded as the mark of origin for Dublin, while the harp crowned came to be regarded as the Sterling standard mark.

The date letter sequence began in 1638. Dublin used a 20-letter sequence (A to U omitting J) until 1678, when a 23 or 24-letter sequence was introduced (omitting J, V and sometimes I). There was an aborted sequence of A to C in 1717–19. In 1821 a 25-letter sequence was adopted (omitting J). The date letter was changed in June until 1932, since when it has changed in January. As Dublin is in the Irish Republic, it was not affected by the United Kingdom's Hallmarking Act of 1973.

A 1638

B 1639

C 1640

D 1641

E 1642

F 1643

G 1644

H 1645

I 1646

K 1647

L 1648

M 1649

N 1650

O 1651

P 1652

Q 1653

R 1654

S 1655

T 1656

U 1657

a 1658

b 1659

c 1660

d 1661

e 1662

f 1663

g 1664

h 1665

i 1666

k 1667

l 1668

m 1669

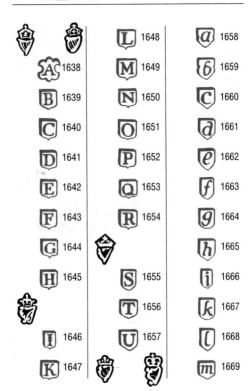

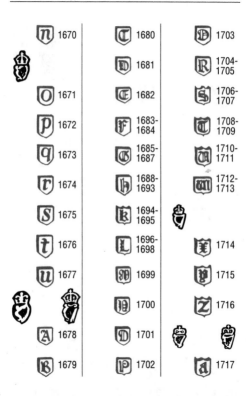

n	1670

o	1671
p	1672
q	1673
r	1674
s	1675
t	1676
u	1677

A	1678
B	1679
C	1680
D	1681
E	1682
F	1683-1684
G	1685-1687
h	1688-1693
k	1694-1695
L	1696-1698
M	1699
N	1700
O	1701
P	1702
Q	1703
R	1704-1705
S	1706-1707
T	1708-1709
U	1710-1711
W	1712-1713

X	1714
Y	1715
Z	1716

a	1717

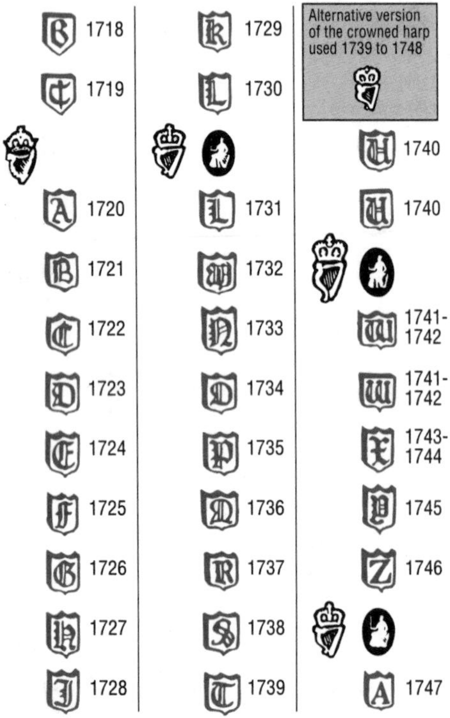
1718
1719
1720
1721
1722
1723
1724
1725
1726
1727
1728
1729
1730
1731
1732
1733
1734
1735
1736
1737
1738
1739
Alternative version of the crowned harp used 1739 to 1748
1740
1740
1741-1742
1741-1742
1743-1744
1745
1746
1747

B 1748

C 1749

D 1750

E 1751

E 1751

F 1752

Alternative version of Hibernia used 1751 to 1752

G 1753

H 1754

I 1757

K 1758

L 1759

M 1760

N 1761

O 1762

P 1763

Q 1764

R 1765

S 1766

T 1767

U 1768

W 1769

X 1770

Y 1771

Z 1772

A 1773

B 1774

C 1775

D 1776

E 1777

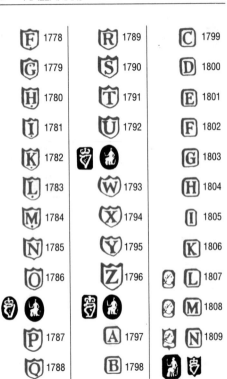

F 1778

G 1779

H 1780

I 1781

K 1782

L 1783

M 1784

N 1785

O 1786

P 1787

Q 1788

R 1789

S 1790

T 1791

U 1792

W 1793

X 1794

Y 1795

Z 1796

A 1797

B 1798

C 1799

D 1800

E 1801

F 1802

G 1803

H 1804

I 1805

K 1806

 L 1807

 M 1808

 N 1809

1810
1811
1812
1813
1814
1815
1816
1817
1818
1819
1820
1821
1822
1823
1824
1825
1825
1826
1827
1828
1829
1830
1831
1832
1833
1834
1835
1836

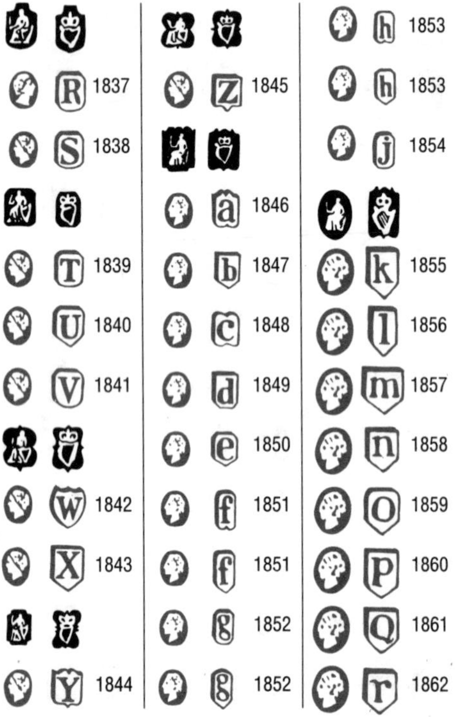

R 1837
S 1838
T 1839
U 1840
V 1841
W 1842
X 1843
Y 1844
Z 1845
a 1846
b 1847
c 1848
d 1849
e 1850
f 1851
f 1851
g 1852
g 1852
h 1853
h 1853
j 1854
k 1855
l 1856
m 1857
n 1858
O 1859
P 1860
Q 1861
r 1862

S 1863
t 1864
u 1865
V 1866
W 1867
X 1868
Y 1869
Z 1870
A 1871
B 1872
C 1873
D 1874
E 1875
F 1876
G 1877
H 1878
I 1879
K 1880
L 1881
M 1882
N 1883
O 1884
P 1885
Q 1886
R 1887
S 1888
T 1889
U 1890
V 1891
W 1892
X 1893
Y 1894
Z 1895

A	1896
B	1897
C	1898
D	1899
E	1900
F	1901
G	1902
H	1903
I	1904
K	1905
L	1906
M	1907
N	1908
O	1909
P	1910
Q	1911
R	1912
S	1913
T	1914
U	1915

A	1916
b	1917
c	1918
d	1919
e	1920
f	1921
g	1922
h	1923
i	1924
k	1925
l	1926
m	1927
n	1928
o	1929
p	1930-1931

The date letter was changed on 1 June up to 1931. The Q of 1932 and all subsequent letters began on 1 January

Q 1932

R 1933

S 1934

T 1935

U 1936

V 1937

W 1938

X 1939

Y 1940

Z 1941

A 1942

B 1943

C 1944

D 1945

E 1946

F 1947

G 1948

H 1949

I 1950

J 1951

K 1952

L 1953

M 1954

N 1955

O 1956

P 1957

Q 1958

R 1959

S 1960

T 1961

U 1962

V 1963

W 1964

X 1965

 Y 1966

Special 'Sword of Light' mark used to commemorate 50th anniversary of 1916 Rising, in 1966

Z 1967

a 1968

b 1969

c 1970

d 1971

e 1972

F 1973

Special mark used in 1973 showing Gleninsheen Collar, to commemorate Ireland's entry into the EEC

g 1974

h 1975

i 1976

l 1977

m 1978

n 1979

o 1980

p 1981

R 1982

S 1983

t 1984

u 1985

1986

1987

Special shield used in 1987 to commemorate the 350th anniversary of the Goldsmith's Company of Dublin

1988

Special mark used in 1988 to commemorate the Dublin City Milennium Year

1989

1990

1991

1992

1993

1994

DUBLIN MAKERS' MARKS

AB	Alexander Brown
AL	Antony Lefebure
AR	Alexander Richards
BM	Bartholomew Mosse
CM	Charles Marsh
CT	Christopher Thompson
DE	Daniel Egan
DK	David King
EB	Edward Barrett
EC	E Crofton
EF	Esther Forbes
EJ	Edmund Johnson
EP	Edward Pome
GA	George Alcock
GW	George Wheatley
HM	Henry Matthews
IB	John Buckton
IC	John Cuthbert or John Christie
IF	John Fry
IH	John Hamilton
II	Joseph Jackson
IL	John Laughlin
ILB	John Le Bas
IP	John Pittar
IS	James Scott
JD	James Douglas
JP	John Power
J.P	John Pittar
JS	James Smythe
MH	Michael Hewitson
MN	Michael Nowlan
MW	Matthew West
PM	Patrick Moore
PW	Peter Walsh
RC	Robert Calderwood
RS	Richard Sawyer
RW	Richard Williams or Robert William
SN	Samuel Neville
SW	Samuel Walker
TJ	Thomas Jones
TK	Thomas Kinslea
TP	Thomas Parker
TS	Thomas Slade
TW	Thomas Walker
TWY+	Edward Twycross
WA	William Archdall
WC	William Cummins
WL	William Lawson
WN	William Nowlan
WR	William Rose
WW	William Williamson

NEWCASTLE

Silver was assayed in Newcastle from the mid 17th century, becoming systematic in 1702. Newcastle is known for domestic silver, tankards and two-handled cups. A curiosity of Newcastle is the presence of three known women silversmiths.

The town mark depicted three separate castles. From 1702 to 1719, the Britannia mark and the lion's head erased were in use. From 1720, these were replaced with the leopard's head and the lion passant. From 1721 to 1727, the lion passant usually faced to the right. The sovereign's head duty mark was used from 1784 to 1883.

The date letter sequence began in 1702. Newcastle used a 19-letter sequence (A to T generally omitting J) until 1759, when a 24-letter sequence was introduced (omitting J and V). The date letter was changed in May. The Newcastle Assay Office was closed in 1884.

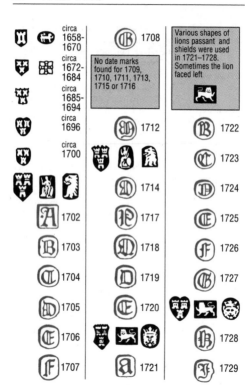

circa 1658-1670

circa 1672-1684

circa 1685-1694

circa 1696

circa 1700

 1702

 1703

 1704

 1705

 1706

 1707

 1708

No date marks found for 1709, 1710, 1711, 1713, 1715 or 1716

 1712

 1714

 1717

 1718

 1719

 1720

 1721

Various shapes of lions passant and shields were used in 1721–1728. Sometimes the lion faced left

 1722

 1723

 1724

 1725

 1726

 1727

 1728

 1729

K 1730
L 1731
M 1732
N 1733
O 1734
P 1735
Q 1736
R 1737
S 1738
T 1739

A 1740
B 1741
C 1742
D 1743
E 1744
F 1745
G 1746
H 1747
I 1748
K 1749
L 1750
M 1751
N 1752
O 1753
P 1754
Q 1755
R 1756
S 1757
S 1758

A 1759
B 1760-1768
C 1769
D 1770
E 1771

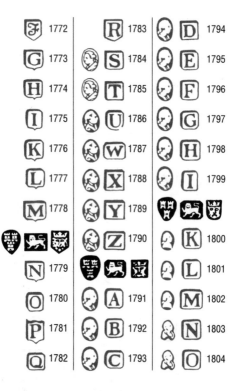

F 1772
G 1773
H 1774
I 1775
K 1776
L 1777
M 1778

N 1779
O 1780
P 1781
Q 1782

R 1783
S 1784
T 1785
U 1786
W 1787
X 1788
Y 1789
Z 1790

A 1791
B 1792
C 1793

D 1794
E 1795
F 1796
G 1797
H 1798
I 1799

K 1800
L 1801
M 1802
N 1803
O 1804

Letter	Year
P	1805
Q	1806
R	1807
S	1808
T	1809
U	1810
W	1811
X	1812
Y	1813
Z	1814

Letter	Year
A	1815
B	1816
C	1817
D	1818
E	1819
F	1820
G	1821
H	1822
I	1823
K	1824
L	1825
M	1826
N	1827
O	1828
P	1829
Q	1830
R	1831
S	1832
T	1833
U	1834
W	1835
X	1836
Y	1837
Z	1838

A	1839
B	1840
C	1841
D	1842
E	1843
F	1844
G	1845

H	1846
I	1847
J	1848
K	1849
L	1850
M	1851
N	1852
O	1853
P	1854
Q	1855
R	1856
S	1857
T	1858
U	1859
W	1860
X	1861
Y	1862
Z	1863

a	1864
b	1865
c	1866
d	1867
e	1868
f	1869
g	1870
h	1871
i	1872

 1873

 1874

 1875

 1876

 1877

 1878

 1879

 1880

 1881

 1882

 1883

Newcastle Assay Office was closed down in 1884

NEWCASTLE MAKERS' MARKS

AK	Alexander Kelty
AR	Anne Robertson
Ba	Francis Batty
Bi	Eli Bilton
Bu	John Buckle
CJR	Christian Reid Junior
CR **DR**	Christian & David Reid
CR **IS**	Christian Reid & John Stoddart
DC	David Crawford
DD	David Darling
DL	Dorothy Langlands
DR	David Reid
FB	Francis Batty
GB	George Bulman
IC	Isaac Cookson
IK	James Kirkup
IL **IR**	John Langlands & John Robertson
IM	John Mitchison
IR	John Robertson
IS	John Stoddart
IW	John Walton
La	John Langwith
L & S	Lister & Sons
MA	Mary Ashworth
Ra	John Ramsay
R & D	Robertson & Darling
RM	Robert Makepeace
RP **RS**	Pinkney & Scott
RS	Robert Scott
TP	Thomas Partis
TS	Thomas Sewill
TW	Thomas Watson
WL	William Lister
WL **CL** **WL**	Lister & Sons
Yo	John Younghusband

CHESTER

From the early 15th century, Chester had a guild of goldsmiths which supervised the making, assaying and selling of plate, although marking was not regulated here until the late 17th century. Chester is known for small items such as beakers and creamers.

The mark of origin was the city arms, of a sword between three wheatsheaves (gerbes). From 1701, this changed to three wheatsheaves halved with three lions halved. From 1701 to 1718, the figure of Britannia and the lion's head erased were used as the standard mark. From 1719, the leopard's head crowned and the lion passant were used. From 1839, the leopard's head was omitted. The sovereign's head duty mark was in use from 1784 to 1890.

The date letter sequence began in 1701, and was of irregular length, varying from 21 to 25 letters. The letter was changed each July until 1839, then in August until 1890, then in July again until the office was closed down in 1962.

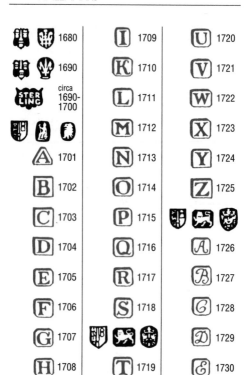

 1680

 1690

circa 1690-1700

A 1701

B 1702

C 1703

D 1704

E 1705

F 1706

G 1707

H 1708

I 1709

K 1710

L 1711

M 1712

N 1713

O 1714

P 1715

Q 1716

R 1717

S 1718

T 1719

U 1720

V 1721

W 1722

X 1723

Y 1724

Z 1725

A 1726

B 1727

C 1728

D 1729

E 1730

F	1731	S	1743	C	1753
G	1732	T	1744	d	1754
H	1733	U	1745	e	1755
I	1734	V	1746	f	1756
K	1735	W	1747	G	1757
L	1736	X	1748	h	1758
M	1737	Y	1749	i	1759
N	1738	Y	1749	k	1760
O	1739	Z	1750	l	1761
P	1740			m	1762
Q	1741	a	1751	n	1763
R	1742	b	1752	o	1764

P	1765
Q	1766
R	1767
S	1768
T	1769
T	1770
U	1771
V	1772
W	1773
X	1774
Y	1775

a	1776
b	1777
c	1778

d	1779
e	1780
f	1781
g	1782
h	1783

i	1784
k	1785
l	1786
m	1787
n	1788
o	1789
p	1790
q	1791
r	1792
s	1793
t	1794
u	1795
v	1796

Date letter	Year
A	1797
B	1798
C	1799

Date letter	Year
D	1800
E	1801
F	1802
G	1803
H	1804
I	1805
K	1806
L	1807
M	1808
N	1809
O	1810
P	1811
Q	1812
R	1813
S	1814
T	1815
U	1816
V	1817

Date letter	Year
A	1818
B	1819
C	1820
D	1821
D	1822

Date letter	Year
E	1823
F	1824
G	1825
H	1826
I	1827
K	1828
L	1829

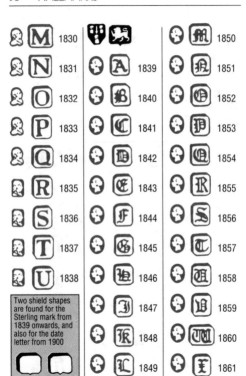

Date letter	Year
M	1830
N	1831
O	1832
P	1833
Q	1834
R	1835
S	1836
T	1837
U	1838
𝔄	1839
𝔅	1840
ℭ	1841
𝔇	1842
𝔈	1843
𝔉	1844
𝔊	1845
ℌ	1846
ℑ	1847
𝔎	1848
𝔏	1849
𝔐	1850
𝔑	1851
𝔒	1852
𝔓	1853
𝔔	1854
ℜ	1855
𝔖	1856
𝔗	1857
𝔘	1858
𝔙	1859
𝔚	1860
𝔛	1861

Two shield shapes are found for the Sterling mark from 1839 onwards, and also for the date letter from 1900

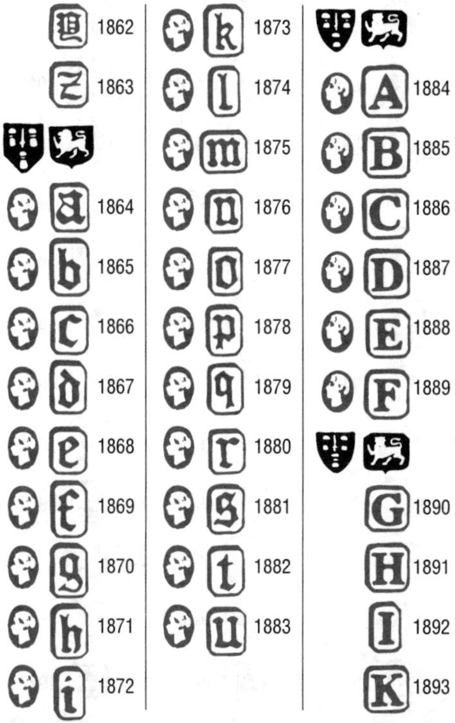

y 1862
z 1863
a 1864
b 1865
c 1866
d 1867
e 1868
f 1869
g 1870
h 1871
i 1872
k 1873
l 1874
m 1875
n 1876
o 1877
p 1878
q 1879
r 1880
s 1881
t 1882
u 1883
A 1884
B 1885
C 1886
D 1887
E 1888
F 1889
G 1890
H 1891
I 1892
K 1893

L 1894
M 1895
N 1896
O 1897
P 1898
Q 1899
R 1900

A 1901
B 1902
C 1903
D 1904
E 1905
F 1906
G 1907
H 1908
I 1909
K 1910
L 1911
M 1912
N 1913
O 1914
P 1915
Q 1916
R 1917
S 1918
T 1919
U 1920
V 1921
W 1922
X 1923
Y 1924
Z 1925

a 1926
b 1927

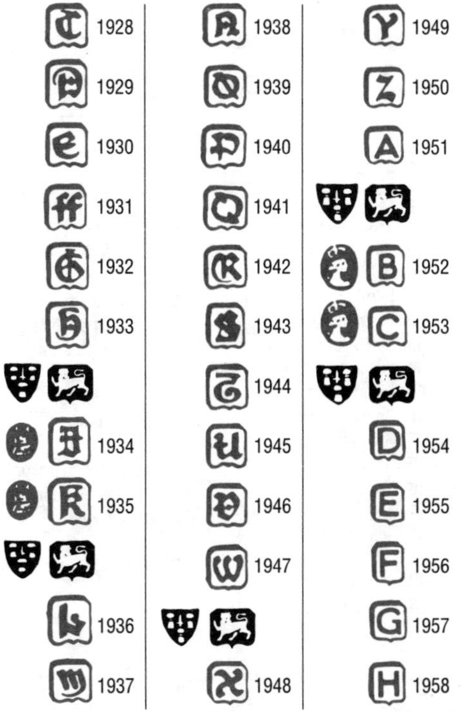
1928
1929
1930
1931
1932
1933
1934
1935
1936
1937
1938
1939
1940
1941
1942
1943
1944
1945
1946
1947
1948
1949
1950
1951
1952
1953
1954
1955
1956
1957
1958

	1959
	1960
	1961
	1962

Chester Assay Office closed in August 1962

CHESTER MAKERS' MARKS

B & F	Matthew Boulton & James Fothergill
Bi	Charles Bird
BP	Benjamin Pemberton
Bu	Nathaniel Bullen
Du	Bartholomew Duke
EM	Edward Maddock
FB	Francis Butt
GL	George Lowe
GR	George Roberts
GW	George Walker
IB	James Barton
IG	John Gilbert
IL TL	John & Thomas Lowe
IR	John Richards
IW	Joseph Walley
JA	John Adamson
JC	James Conway or John Coakley
JL	John Lowe
JS	John Sutters
NC	Nicholas Cunliffe
Pe	Peter Pemberton
RG	Robert Green
RI	Robert Jones
RL	Robert Lowe
RP	Richard Pike
RR	Richard Richardson
TM	Thomas Maddock
WH	William Hull
WP	William Pugh
WR	William Richardson

GLASGOW

Silver was assayed in Glasgow from the late 17th century, although in the years 1784–1819 Glasgow silverware was mainly assayed in Edinburgh. In the latter year the Glasgow Goldsmiths' Company was formed and several changes were made in the marks. The Glasgow mark of origin was a tree with a bird in the upper branches, a bell hanging from a lower branch and a fish (with a ring in its mouth) laid across the trunk. From 1819, a lion rampant was adopted as the Sterling standard mark, and in 1914 the Scottish thistle was added. Also from 1819, the Britannia standard (and appropriate mark) were in optional use. Up to 1784, the maker's mark was stamped twice, once on each side of the mark of origin. The sovereign's head duty mark was used from 1819 to 1890.

The date letter sequence began in 1681. After about the first 25 years, regular cycles were abandoned and the letters 's' and 'o' were commonly used until 1819, when a full 26-letter sequence was introduced. The date letter was changed annually in July.

The Glasgow Assay Office closed in 1964.

Date letters were used in 1681-1709, but then not again until 1819

The maker's mark was stamped on both sides of the Glasgow town mark up to 1784

 1681

 1683

 1685

 1689

 1690

 1694

 1696

 1698

 1699

 1700

 1701

 1704

 1705

 circa 1707

 circa 1709

 circa 1717

The letter S was used probably as a Sterling mark

 circa 1728

 circa 1734

 circa 1743

 circa 1747

 circa 1756

 circa 1757

 circa 1758

 circa 1763

 circa 1773

 circa 1773

 circa 1776

 circa 1780

 circa 1781

 circa 1783

S	circa 1784
	1811
—	—
A	1819
—	—
B	1820
C	1821
D	1822
E	1823
F	1824
G	1825
H	1826
I	1827
J	1828
K	1829
L	1830
M	1831
N	1832
O	1833
P	1834
Q	1835
R	1836
—	—
S	1837
T	1838
U	1839
V	1840
W	1841
X	1842
Y	1843
Z	1844
—	—
A	1845
B	1846
C	1847
D	1848

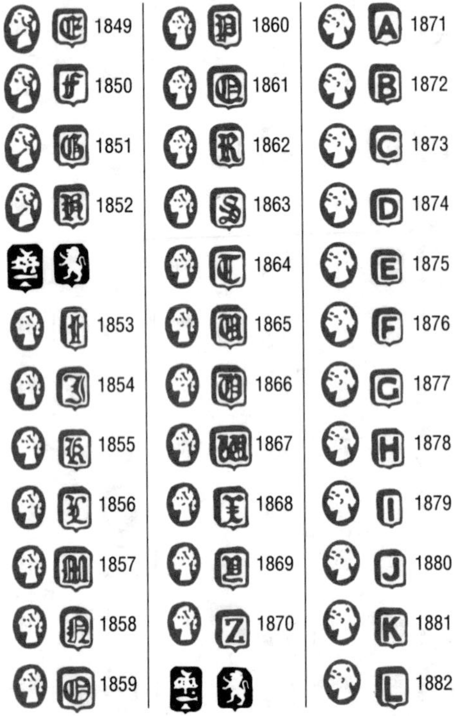
1849
1850
1851
1852
1853
1854
1855
1856
1857
1858
1859
1860
1861
1862
1863
1864
1865
1866
1867
1868
1869
1870
1871
1872
1873
1874
1875
1876
1877
1878
1879
1880
1881
1882

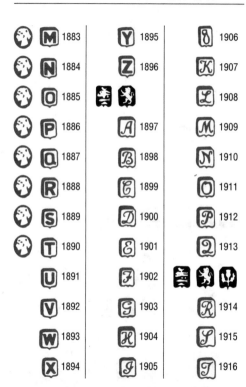

M 1883	Y 1895	𝒥 1906
N 1884	Z 1896	𝒦 1907
O 1885		ℒ 1908
P 1886	𝒜 1897	ℳ 1909
Q 1887	ℬ 1898	𝒩 1910
R 1888	𝒞 1899	𝒪 1911
S 1889	𝒟 1900	𝒫 1912
T 1890	ℰ 1901	𝒬 1913
U 1891	ℱ 1902	
V 1892	𝒢 1903	ℛ 1914
W 1893	ℋ 1904	𝒮 1915
X 1894	ℐ 1905	𝒯 1916

u 1917
v 1918
w 1919
x 1920
y 1921
z 1922

a 1923
b 1924
c 1925
d 1926
e 1927

f 1928
g 1929
h 1930
i 1931
j 1932
k 1933

l 1934

m 1935

n 1936
o 1937

p 1938
q 1939
r 1940
s 1941
t 1942
u 1943
v 1944
w 1945
x 1946
y 1947
z 1948

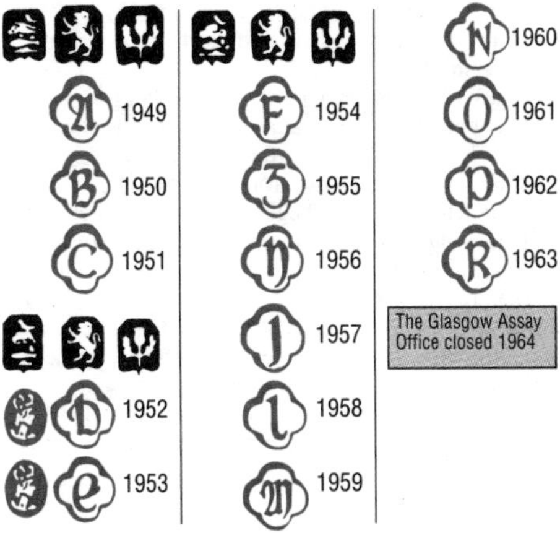
1949
1950
1951
1952
1953
1954
1955
1956
1957
1958
1959
1960
1961
1962
1963

The Glasgow Assay Office closed 1964

GLASGOW MAKERS' MARKS

AM	Alexander Mitchell
A & T	Aird & Thompson
DCR	Duncan Rait
DMcD	David McDonald
JC	James Crichton
JL	John Law
JM	John Mitchell or J Murray
LFN	Luke Newlands
PA	Peter Arthur
RG & S	Robert Gray & Sons
WP	William Parkins

BIRMINGHAM

The Birmingham Assay Office opened in 1773, after which the city grew quickly in importance as a centre for silversmithing.

The mark of origin is an anchor (struck lying on its side for gold and platinum). It appeared very consistently with the lion passant standard mark. The sovereign's head duty mark was in use from 1784 to 1890.

The date letter sequence began in 1773 (in which year the letter A appeared in three different shapes of shield). Birmingham used 25 and 26-letter sequences alternately (omitting J). The date letter was changed in July until 1975, since when all British date letters have been standardized and changed on 1 January. In the same year, platinum was first assayed here.

A special commemorative mark was struck in 1973 to mark the bicentenary of the Birmingham Assay Office. The Office is still in operation today.

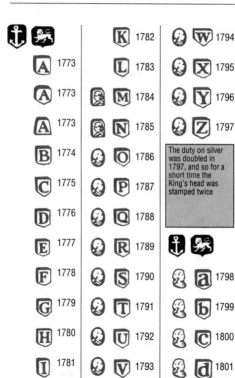

Letter	Year
A	1773
A	1773
A	1773
B	1774
C	1775
D	1776
E	1777
F	1778
G	1779
H	1780
I	1781
K	1782
L	1783
M	1784
N	1785
O	1786
P	1787
Q	1788
R	1789
S	1790
T	1791
U	1792
V	1793
W	1794
X	1795
Y	1796
Z	1797

The duty on silver was doubled in 1797, and so for a short time the King's head was stamped twice

Letter	Year
a	1798
b	1799
c	1800
d	1801

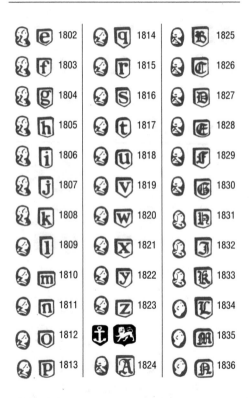

e	1802
f	1803
g	1804
h	1805
i	1806
j	1807
k	1808
l	1809
m	1810
n	1811
o	1812
p	1813
q	1814
r	1815
s	1816
t	1817
u	1818
v	1819
w	1820
x	1821
y	1822
z	1823

A	1824
B	1825
C	1826
D	1827
E	1828
F	1829
G	1830
H	1831
I	1832
K	1833
L	1834
M	1835
N	1836

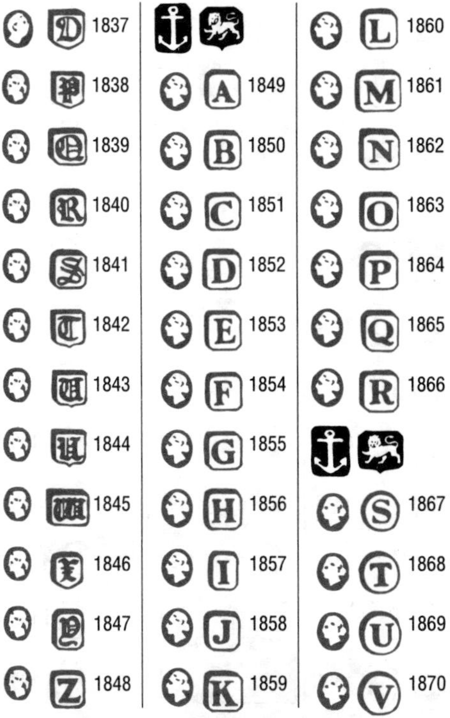
1837
1838
1839
1840
1841
1842
1843
1844
1845
1846
1847
1848
1849
1850
1851
1852
1853
1854
1855
1856
1857
1858
1859
1860
1861
1862
1863
1864
1865
1866
1867
1868
1869
1870

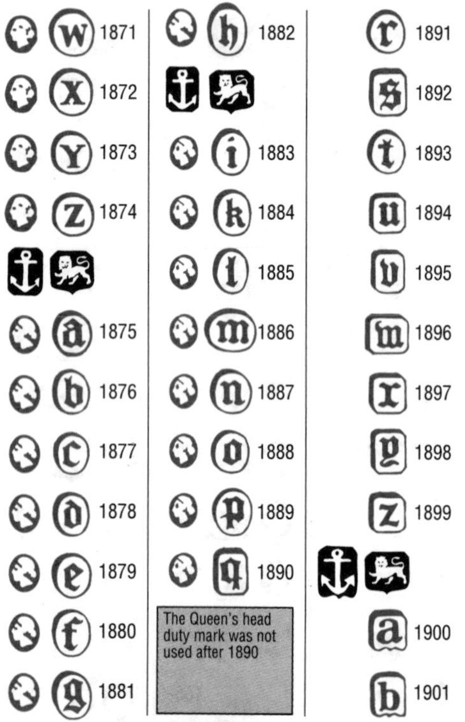

The Queen's head duty mark was not used after 1890

c 1902
d 1903
e 1904
f 1905
g 1906
h 1907
i 1908
k 1909
l 1910
m 1911
n 1912
o 1913

p 1914
q 1915
r 1916
s 1917

t 1918
u 1919
v 1920
w 1921
x 1922
y 1923
z 1924

A 1925
B 1926
C 1927
D 1928
E 1929
F 1930
G 1931
H 1932
J 1933

 K 1934

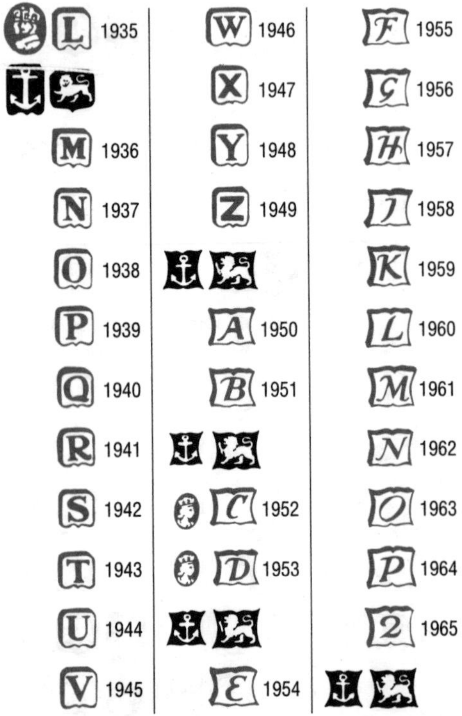
L 1935
M 1936
N 1937
O 1938
P 1939
Q 1940
R 1941
S 1942
T 1943
U 1944
V 1945
W 1946
X 1947
Y 1948
Z 1949
A 1950
B 1951
C 1952
D 1953
E 1954
F 1955
G 1956
H 1957
J 1958
K 1959
L 1960
M 1961
N 1962
O 1963
P 1964
Q 1965

 1966

 1967

 1968

 1969

 1970

 1971

 1972

In 1973 the bicentenary of the Birmingham Assay Office was commemorated by a special town mark

 1973

 1974

New letter sequence commenced from 1 January 1975, in accordance with the Hallmarking Act passed in 1973

 1975

 1976

 1977

 1978

 1979

 1980

 1981

 1982

 1983

 1984

 1985

 1986

 1987

 1988

 1989

 1990

 1991

 1992

 1993

 1994

BIRMINGHAM MAKERS' MARKS

C & B	Cocks & Bettridge
E & CoLd	Elkington & Co
EM & Co	Elkington Mason & Co
ES	Edward Smith
ET	Edward Thomasson
FC	Francis Clark
GU	George Unite
GW	Gervase Wheeler
H & T	Hilliard & Thomasson
IB	John Bettridge
IS	John Shaw
IT	Joseph Taylor
JW	Joseph Willmore
L & Co	John Lawrence & Co
MB	Matthew Boulton
MB IF	Matthew Boulton & John Fothergill
ML	Matthew Linwood
NM	Nathaniel Mills
P & T	William Postan & George Tye
REA	Robinson, Edkins & Aston
SP	Samuel Pemberton
T & P	Joseph Taylor & John Perry
TS	Thomas Shaw
TW	Thomas Willmore
WF	William Fowke
Y & W	Yapp & Woodward

SHEFFIELD

The Assay Office was opened in 1773. Sheffield is best known for the production of candlesticks.

The mark of origin on Sheffield silver was the crown until 1975, since when it has been a York rose. The standard mark was a lion passant. The sovereign's head duty mark was in use from 1784 to 1890.

From 1780 to 1853, small items were marked with a special stamp on which the crown mark of origin and the date letter were combined.

The application of date letters began in September 1773 with the letter E, changing every July. The choice of letter was quite random until 1824, when Sheffield began to use a regular 25-letter alphabetical sequence (omitting J). In 1975, the standard British date letter sequence was imposed, with the letter being changed on 1 January each year. In the same year, platinum was first assayed at Sheffield.

The Sheffield Assay Office is still in operation.

 1773

 1774

 1775

 1776

 1777

 1778

 1779

For alternative marks used on small objects from 1780 to 1853, see pages 123-125

 1780

In the period 1780 to 1823, the crown and lion passant varied slightly, eg:

Also varied in years 1824–43, but crown is in a square shield

 1781

 1782

 1783

 1784

 1785

 1786

 1787

 1788

 1789

 1790

 1791

 1792

 1793

 1794

 1795

 1796

 1797

From 15 July 1797 for nine months, the duty on silver was doubled and so the King's head was stamped twice

V	1798	L	1810	Z	1822
E	1799	C	1811	U	1823
N	1800	D	1812	a	1824
H	1801	R	1813	b	1825
M	1802	W	1814	c	1826
F	1803	O	1815	d	1827
G	1804	T	1816	e	1828
B	1805	X	1817	f	1829
A	1806	I	1818	g	1830
S	1807	V	1819	h	1831
P	1808	Q	1820	k	1832
K	1809	Y	1821	l	1833

m 1834
P 1835
q 1836
r 1837
S 1838
t 1839
u 1840
V 1841
X 1842
Z 1843

A 1844
B 1845
C 1846
D 1847
E 1848
F 1849
G 1850
H 1851
I 1852
K 1853
L 1854
M 1855
N 1856
O 1857
P 1858
R 1859
S 1860
T 1861
U 1862
V 1863
W 1864
X 1865
Y 1866
Z 1867

1868
1869
1870
1871
1872

From 1780 to 1853, the combined crown and date letters shown below were used on small objects assayed at the Sheffield Office

1780
1781
1782

1783
1784
1785
1786
1787
1788
1789
1790
1791
1792
1793
1794

1795
1796
1797
1798
1799
1800
1801
1802
1803
1804
1805
1806

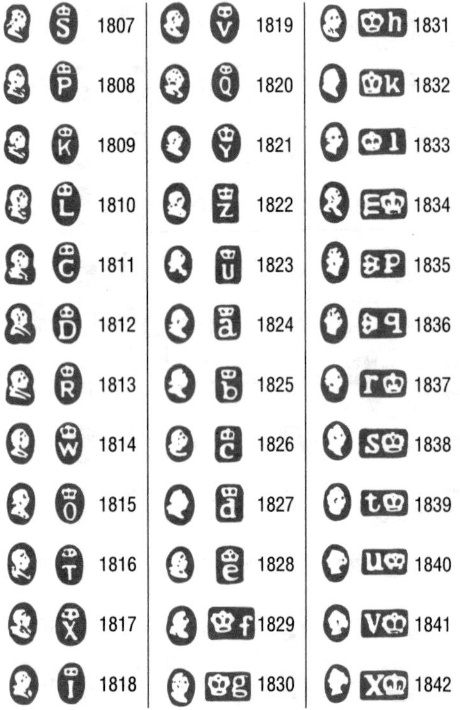
1807
1808
1809
1810
1811
1812
1813
1814
1815
1816
1817
1818
1819
1820
1821
1822
1823
1824
1825
1826
1827
1828
1829
1830
1831
1832
1833
1834
1835
1836
1837
1838
1839
1840
1841
1842

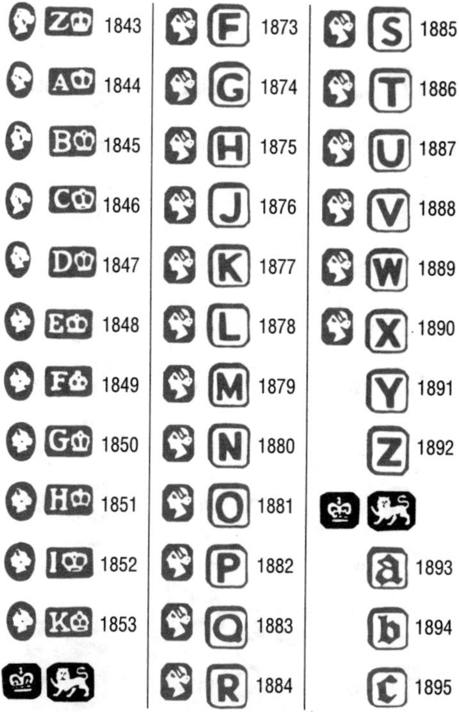
Z 1843
A 1844
B 1845
C 1846
D 1847
E 1848
F 1849
G 1850
H 1851
I 1852
K 1853
F 1873
G 1874
H 1875
J 1876
K 1877
L 1878
M 1879
N 1880
O 1881
P 1882
Q 1883
R 1884
S 1885
T 1886
U 1887
V 1888
W 1889
X 1890
Y 1891
Z 1892
a 1893
b 1894
c 1895

d 1896
e 1897
f 1898
g 1899
h 1900
i 1901
k 1902
l 1903
m 1904
n 1905
o 1906
p 1907

q 1908
r 1909
s 1910
t 1911
u 1912
v 1913
w 1914
x 1915
y 1916
z 1917

a 1918

b 1919
c 1920
d 1921
e 1922
f 1923
g 1924
h 1925
i 1926
k 1927
l 1928
m 1929
n 1930

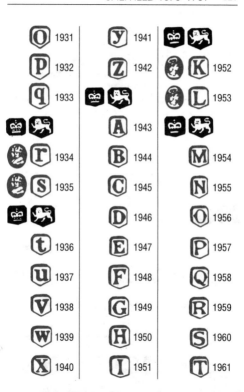

O 1931

P 1932

q 1933

 r 1934

 S 1935

t 1936

u 1937

V 1938

W 1939

X 1940

y 1941

Z 1942

A 1943

B 1944

C 1945

D 1946

E 1947

F 1948

G 1949

H 1950

I 1951

 K 1952

 L 1953

M 1954

N 1955

O 1956

P 1957

Q 1958

R 1959

S 1960

T 1961

U 1962

V 1963

W 1964

X 1965

Y 1966

Z 1967

A 1968

B 1969

C 1970

D 1971

E 1972

Œ 1973

The 1773 date letter was used in 1973 to commemorate the Sheffield Assay Office bicentenary

G 1974

New letter sequence commenced from 1 January 1975, in accordance with the Hallmarking Act passed in 1973

A 1975

B 1976

 C 1977

D 1978

E 1979

F 1980

G 1981

H 1982

I 1983

K 1984

L 1985

M 1986

N 1987

 1988

 1989

 1990

 1991

 1992

 1993

 1994

SHEFFIELD MAKERS' MARKS

AH	Aaron Hadfield
DH & Co	Daniel Holy & Co
D & S	Dixon & Sons
GA & Co	George Ashforth & Co
GE & Co	George Eadon & Co
HA	Henry Archer & Co
H & H	Howard & Hawksworth
HE & Co	Hawksworth, Eyre & Co
HT	Henry Tudor
HW & Co	Henry Wilkinson & Co
IG & Co	John Green & Co
IH & Co	J Hoyland & Co
IL	John Law
IP & Co	John Parsons & Co
IR & Co	John Roberts & Co
ITY & Co	John T Younge & Co
IW & Co	John Winter & Co
JB	James Burbury
JC NC	J & N Creswick
JD & S	James Dixon & Sons
JR	J Round & Son
MF RC	Fenton, Creswick & Co
MH & Co	Martin Hall & Co
NS & Co	Nathaniel Smith & Co
RM	Richard Morton
RM & Co	Richard Morton & Co
RM EH	Remy Martin & Edward Hall
S & N	Stafford & Newton
SR & Co	Samuel Roberts & Co
T & IS	T & I Settle
TJ NC	TJ & N Creswick
WD	William Damant
WF AF	Fordham & Faulkner
W & H	Walker & Hall

HALLMARKS ON GOLD

Gold marks are much the same as silver marks. A set of gold hallmarks usually consists of four: a mark of origin, a standard mark, a date letter and a maker's mark. Duty marks and commemorative marks are also found at certain periods, just as on silver. Many changes have occurred over the years, most notably with the 1973 Hallmarking Act, which standardized hallmarking at all British assay offices.

Carat numbers

The carat number is the traditional measurement of purity for gold. One carat is equal to one twenty-fourth of the weight of an object. Thus a 22 carat object contains 22 parts gold and two parts alloy. A 9 carat object contains nine parts gold and 15 parts alloy.

Standard marks on British gold

Before 1363, a leopard's head crowned (see **1** on table overleaf) denoted the gold standard of $19^1/_5$ carat, and would be found near the mark of origin on an object. From 1363 onwards, the maker's mark was added to these marks. In 1477, the standard was reduced to 18 carat, but was denoted by the same mark (**1**). In 1478, date letters were first added, as on silver. 1544 saw the first change in the standard mark, to the lion passant (**2**). In 1575 the standard was increased to 22 carat, but using the same mark. In 1798, the 18 carat standard was reintroduced as an alternative, with new marks of a crown and a figure 18 (**3**). The 22 carat standard mark remained the lion passant. From 1844 the lion passant mark was replaced as the standard mark for 22 carat

1		$19^{1}/_{5}$ carat 18 carat	c1300–1476 1477–1544
2		18 carat 22 carat	1544–1574 1575–1843
3		18 carat	1798–1974
4		22 carat	1844–1974
5		15 carat	1854–1931
6		12 carat	1854–1931
7		9 carat	1854–1931
8		14 carat	1932-1974
9		9 carat	1932–1974
Scotland			
10		18 carat	Edinburgh 1759–1974
11		22 carat	Glasgow 1914–1974

gold by a crown and the figure 22 (**4**). In 1854 three additional lower standards of 15 (**5**), 12 (**6**) and 9 (**7**) carat were introduced, with their standard marks as shown. This was the first time that millesimal numbers (giving the parts of gold per thousand) were used. The

15 and 12 carat standards were dropped in 1932, and replaced by 14 carat (**8**), along with a new mark for 9 carat (**9**). In Scotland up to 31 December 1974, the thistle was used (instead of the crown used in England), with the numbers 18 (**10**) or 22 (**11**) for the 18 or 22 carat gold standards respectively.

Standard marks under the Hallmarking Act 1973

From 1 January 1975, gold standard marks were made the same at all English and Scottish assay offices, becoming a crown mark next to the millesimal value.

22 carat

14 carat

18 carat

9 carat

Standard marks on Irish gold

At Dublin from 1637 to 1784, the same marks as used for silver were used for gold, with the standard being set at 22 carat and the mark a harp crowned (**a**). From 1784, there were three standards of 22 (**b**), 20 (**c**) and

a  22 carat 1637–1784

b 

22 carat 1784–today

c 

20 carat 1784–today

d 

18 carat 1784–today

e 

14 carat 1935–today

f 

9 carat 1854–today

18 (**d**) carat, each using a symbol and number as its mark, as shown. From 1854 three additional lower standards were introduced, of 15 carat (stamped '15' and '.625'), 12 carat (stamped '12' and '.5') and 9 carat (**f**). In 1935, the 15 and 12 carat standards were replaced with 14 carat (**e**), giving the five standards of 22, 20 (rare), 18, 14 and 9 carat found today.

Marks of origin on British and Irish gold

The marks of origin placed on gold by the various assay offices have generally been the same as those placed on silver. However, Birmingham and Dublin have always turned their usual mark on its side in the case of gold. When Sheffield first assayed gold in 1904, it was already using a crown as its town mark for silver. So, to avoid confusion with the crown used as the British standard mark for gold, Sheffield adopted a rose as its town mark on gold. Since 1975 it has used the same York rose on silver and gold alike (see table).

Other marks

Date letters, makers' marks, commemorative marks and duty marks have always been applied to gold just as to silver. Similarly, convention marks for gold follow the same system as on silver (see page 15).

Marks of origin on British and Irish gold

London
Birmingham
Sheffield
Edinburgh
Dublin

IMPORTED GOLD

Standard marks on imported gold

From 1904 to 1974, combined carat and millesimal marks were used. Since 1975, simple millesimal marks have been used.

Carat	1904–1932	1932–1974	From 1974
22	22 ·916	22 ·916	916
18	18 ·75	18 ·750	750
15	15 ·625	—	—
14	—	14 ·585	585
12	12 ·5	—	—
9	9 ·375	9 ·375	375

Marks of origin on imported gold

From 1876 to 1904, each assay office used its usual mark of origin for gold plus a letter F in an oval or rectangle. From 1904, each office adopted a special mark (as shown below).

	All offices	(1876–1904)
	Birmingham	(1904–today)
	Chester	(1904–1962)
	Dublin	(1904–1906)
	Dublin	(1906–today)
	Edinburgh	(1904–today)
	Glasgow	(1904–1906)
	Glasgow	(1906–1964)
	London	(1904–1906)
	London	(1906–today)
	Sheffield	(1904–1906)
	Sheffield	(1906–today)

PLATINUM

Most platinum comes from Latin America. The metal was unknown in Europe before 1600, and it was not until the 19th century that it was worked into jewellery. In Britain there was no legal requirement to mark platinum until 1975, when the Hallmarking Act of 1973 came into force. There is now a single standard for platinum, set at 950 parts per thousand, and all items weighing more than 0.5 grams must be marked.

As with silver and gold, a set of hallmarks for British platinum consists of four elements: a maker's mark, the standard mark, a mark of origin and a date letter. The platinum standard mark is an orb with a cross on top. Imported platinum also bears four marks, but the standard mark is the figure 950, and the mark of origin used by each assay office has the same symbol as placed on imported silver or gold, but contained in a distinctive roof-shaped shield in the case of platinum.

	British		**Imported**	
	Origin	Standard	Origin	Standard
London				950
Birmingham				950
Sheffield				950
Edinburgh				950

2. Old Sheffield Plate

Old Sheffield Plate was manufactured for about 100 years. It was accidentally discovered in 1742 by Thomas Boulsover, who fused a thin layer of silver onto copper to make an instantly appealing new product that looked like silver but cost a fraction of its price. He used it mainly for small objects such as buttons, snuff boxes and buckles. He tried to keep his process a secret, but it was soon copied and used for everything from candlesticks to teapots.

A problem was soon discovered with Sheffield Plate, in that the silver would wear away and reveal the copper beneath. So from around 1760, a greater proportion of silver to copper was used, although precise standards varied greatly.

The manufacturers of Old Sheffield Plate were often also silversmiths, and all the makers followed popular styles of silverware for their designs. The demise of Old Sheffield Plate was brought about in the 1840s by a new process called British plate, which itself was replaced later in the century by the even cheaper electroplating process.

Marks on Old Sheffield Plate

There are a number of problems with identifying and dating Old Sheffield Plate by its marks. For instance, a precise date cannot be given, as the makers' marks appeared without the date letter that is struck on all solid silver. And, because of the resemblance they bore to silver marks, marks on Sheffield plate were made illegal altogether in 1773. From 1784, marks were again permitted, but had to be easily distinguishable from silver marks. Some manufacturers ignored the new law and used marks looking quite similar to those on silver, some obeyed the letter of the law and others did not bother to use a mark at all.

From 1765 to 1825, the crown was used by some makers as a guarantee of quality. From 1820, some makers stamped an identification such as 'Best Sheffield Heavy Silver Plating' on their products.

Other guidelines

After 1835, electroplating often simulated Sheffield Plate, and later pieces are often passed off as Sheffield Plate even though made by a quite different process.

One reliable way of telling Old Sheffield Plate from its imitators is by its colour – it has a soft, slightly bluish glow. The old plating process meant that hollow objects had a seam on them, whereas electro-plating covers a piece seamlessly.

The words 'Sheffield Plated' when marked on an object actually mean it would have been electroplated – the opposite of what one would expect. Something else to watch out for is the foreign competition: cheap French imports of much inferior quality. These are only lightly silvered and have a reddish glow, rather than the bluish one of the genuine article.

MAKERS' MARKS ON OLD SHEFFIELD PLATE

The makers' marks illustrated on pages 140–151 are a selection from the many that are to be found.

Key to abbreviations:

B = Birmingham L = London
N = Nottingham S = Sheffield

1 

2 

3 

4 

5 

6 

7 

8 

9 

10 

11 

12 

13 

14 

15 

16 

MARKS WITH FULL NAMES

1 Lea, Abner Cowel. 1808 B.
2 Goodman, Alexander & Co. 1800 S.
3 Allgood, John. 1812 B.
4 Ashforth, G & Co. 1784 S.
5 Ashley. 1816 B.
6 Askew. 1828 N.
7 Banister, William. 1808 B.
8 Barnet.
9 Beldon, George. 1809 S.
10 Beldon, Hoyland & Co. 1785 S.
11 Best, Henry. 1814 B.
12 Best & Wastidge. 1816 S.
13 Bishop, Thomas. 1830.
14 Boulton. 1784 B.
15 Bradshaw, Joseph. 1822 B.
16 Brittain, Wilkinson & Brownill. 1785 S.
17 Butts, T. 1807 B.
18 Causer, John Fletcher. 1824 B.
19 Cheston, Thomas. 1809 B.
20 Child, Thomas. 1821 B.
21 Needham, C. 1821 S.
22 Cope, Charles Gretter. 1817 B.
23 Corn, James & Sheppard, John. 1819 B.
24 Cracknall, John. 1814 B.
25 Creswick, Thomas & James. 1811 S.
26 Holy, Daniel, Parker & Co. 1804 S.

17

BUTTS

18

CAUSER

19

Ches-
ton

20

CHILD

21

C NEEDHAM
MAKER
SHEFFIELD

22

COPE

23

CORN
& CO

24

CRACK
NALL

25

CRESWICKS

26

DAN HOLY
PARKER & Co

1 DANL HOLY WILKINSON & Co
2 DAVIS
3 D·HORTON
4 DEAKIN SMITH & Co
5 DIXON & Co
6 DUNN
7 E GOODWIN
8 ELL ER BY
9 F·MOORE
10 FOX·PROCTOR PASMORE·& Co
11 FREETH
12 FROGGATT COLDWELL & LEAN
13 GAINSFORD
14 GARNETT
15 GIBBS
16 GIL BERT
17 GREEN
18 HALL

MARKS WITH FULL NAMES (continued)

1 Holy, Daniel, Wilkinson & Co. 1784 S.
2 Davis, John. 1816 B.
3 Horton, David. 1808 B.
4 Deakin, Smith & Co. 1785 S.
5 Dixon & Co. 1784 B.
6 Dunn, G B. 1810 B.
7 Goodwin, Edward. 1794 S.
8 Ellerby, W. 1803.
9 Moore, F. 1820 B.
10 Fox, Proctor Pasmore & Co. 1784 S.
11 Freeth, Henry. 1784 S.
12 Froggatt, Coldwell & Lean. 1797 S.
13 Gainsford, Robert. 1808 S.
14 Garnett, William. 1803 S.
15 Gibbs, Joseph. 1808 B.
16 Gilbert, John. 1812 B.
17 Green, Joseph. 1807 B.
18 Hall, William. 1820 B.
19 Hancock, Joseph. 1755 S.
20 Hanson, Matthias. 1810 B.
21 Harrison, Joseph. 1809 B.
22 Harwood, T. 1816.
23 Hatfield, Aaron. 1808 S.
24 Hatfield, Aaron. 1810 S.
25 Hill, Daniel & Co. 1806 B.
26 Hinks, Joseph. 1812 B.
27 Hipkiss, J. 1808 B.
28 Hobday, J. 1829.

19 

20 

21 

22 

23 

24 

25 

26 

27 

28 

1 HOLLAND&Cº

2 HOR TON

3 How ard

4 Hutton

5 H WILKINSON&Cº

6 I·DRABBLE &Cº

7 I GREEN&Cº

8 I LOVE & Cº

9 I&S. ROBERTS.

10 I&I WATERHOUSE&Cº

11 J DIXON

12 J. LIN WOOD

13 J·NICHOLDS

14 JONES

15 JOHN·PARSONS&Cº

16 JOHN SON

17 JOR DAN

18 JOSH LILLY

19 KIRKBY· FOR·USE

20 LAW

MARKS WITH FULL NAMES (continued)

1 Holland, H & Co. 1784 B.
2 Horton, John. 1809 B.
3 Howard, Stanley & Thomas. 1809 L.
4 Hutton, William. 1807 B.
5 Wilkinson, Henry & Co. 1836 S.
6 Drabble, James & Co. 1805 S.
7 Green, John & Co. 1799 S.
8 Love, John & Co. 1785 S.
9 Roberts, J & S. 1786 S.
10 Waterhouse, J & Co. 1833 S.
11 Dixon, James & Son. 1835 S.
12 Linwood, John. 1807 B.
13 Nicholds, James. 1808 B.
14 Jones. 1824 B.
15 Parsons, John & Co. 1784 S.
16 Johnson, James. 1812 B.
17 Jordan, Thomas. 1814 B.
18 Lilly, Joseph. 1816 B.
19 Kirkby, Samuel. 1812 S.
20 Law, Thomas. 1758 S.
21 Law, John & Son. 1807 S.
22 Lees, George. 1811 B.
23 Lees, George. 1811 B.
24 Lilly, John. 1815 B.
25 Linwood, John. 1807 B.
26 Linwood, Matthew & Son. 1808 B.
27 Love, Silverside, Darby & Co. 1785 S.
28 Mappin Bros. 1850.

21

22

23

24

25

26

27

28

1 

2 

3 

4 

5 

6 

7 

8 

9 

10 

11 

12 

13 

14 

15 

16 

17 

18 

19 

20 

MARKS WITH FULL NAMES (continued)

1 Meredith, Henry. 1807 B.
2 Moore, Frederick. 1820 B.
3 Morton, Richard & Co. 1785 S.
4 Smith, N & Co. 1784 S.
5 Peake. 1807 B.
6 Pearson, Richard. 1811 B.
7 Pemberton & Mitchell . 1817 B.
8 Pimley, Samuel. 1810 B.
9 Madin, P & Co. 1788 S.
10 Prime, J. 1839.
11 Law, Richard. 1807 B.
12 Roberts & Cadman. 1785 S.
13 Rodgers, Joseph & Sons. 1822 S.
14 Rogers, John. 1819 B.
15 Ryland, William & Sons. 1807 B.
16 Sansom, Thomas & Sons. 1821 S.
17 Scot, William. 1807 B.
18 Younge, S & C & Co. 1813 S.
19 Colmore, S. 1790 S.
20 Evans, Samuel. 1816 B.
21 Shepard, Joseph. 1817 B.
22 Silk, Robert. 1809 B.
23 Silkirk, William. 1807 B.
24 Small, Thomas. 1812 B.
25 Smith, Isaac. 1821 B.
26 Smith, William. 1812 B.
27 Smith & Co. 1784 B.
28 Staniforth, Parkin & Co. 1784 S.

21

22

23

24

25

26

27

28

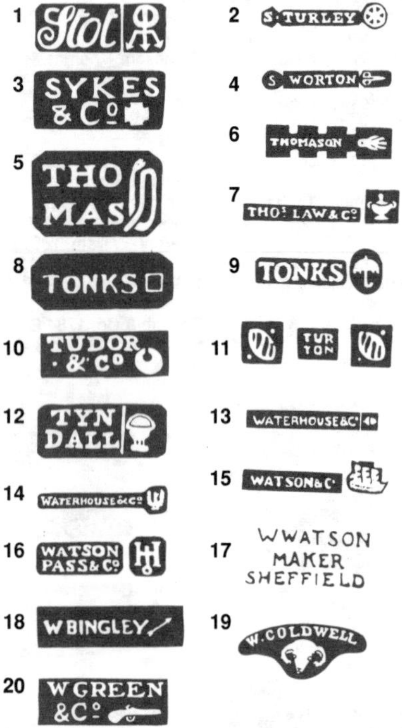
1 Stot
2 S TURLEY
3 SYKES & Cº
4 S WORTON
5 THO MAS
6 THOMASON
7 THOS LAW & Cº
8 TONKS
9 TONKS
10 TUDOR & Cº
11 TUR TON
12 TYN DALL
13 WATERHOUSE & Cº
14 WATERHOUSE & Cº
15 WATSON & Cº
16 WATSON PASS & Cº
17 W WATSON MAKER SHEFFIELD
18 W BINGLEY
19 W. COLDWELL
20 W GREEN & Cº

MARKS WITH FULL NAMES (continued)

1 Stot, Benjamin. 1811 S.
2 Turley, Samuel. 1816 B.
3 Sykes & Co. 1784 S.
4 Worton, Samuel. 1821 B.
5 Thomas, Stephen. 1813 B.
6 Thomason, Edward & Dowler. 1807 B.
7 Law, Thomas & Co. 1784 S.
8 Tonks, Samuel. 1807 B.
9 Tonks & Co. 1824 B.
10 Tudor & Co. 1784 S.
11 Turton, John. 1820 B.
12 Tyndall, Joseph. 1813 B.
13 Waterhouse & Co. 1807 B.
14 Waterhouse, Hatfield & Co. 1836 S.
15 Watson, Fenton & Bradbury. 1795 S.
16 Watson, Pass & Co. 1811 S.
17 Watson, W. 1833 S.
18 Bingley, William. 1787 B.
19 Coldwell, William. 1806 S.
20 Green, W & Co. 1784 S.
21 Hipwood, William. 1809 B.
22 White, John. 1811 B.
23 Willmore, Joseph. 1807 B.
24 Jervis, William. 1789 S.
25 Linwood, William. 1807 B.
26 Markland, William. 1818 B.
27 Newbould, William & Sons. 1804 S.
28 Woodward, William. 1814 B.
29 Wright & Fairbairn. 1809 S.

21 
W·HIP-
WOOD

22 
WHITE

23 
WILLMORE

24 
WJER
VIS

25 
W·LIN
WOOD

26 
W MARKLAND

27 
WM NEWBOULD & SONS

28 
WOOD
WARD

29 
WRIGHT &
FAIRBAIRN

1 

2 

3 

4 

5 

6 

7 

8 

9 

10 

11 

13 

12 

14 

15 

16 

17 

18 

19 

20 

21 

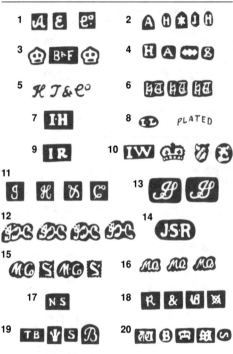

MARKS WITH INITIALS ONLY

1 Ashforth, Ellis & Co. 1770 S.
2 Hatfield, Aaron. 1808 S.
3 Boulton & Fothergill. 1764 S.
4 Atkin, Henry. 1833.
5 Tudor & Leader. 1760 S.
6 Tudor & Leader. 1760 S.
7 Hancock, Joseph. 1755 S.
8 Littlewood, J. 1772 S.
9 Rowbotham, J & Co. 1768 S.
10 Winter, John & Co. 1765 S.
11 Hoyland, John & Co. 1764 S.
12 Hoyland, John & Co. 1764 S.
13 Smallwood, J. 1823.
14 Roberts, Jacob & Samuel. 1765 S.
15 Morton, Richard. 1765 S.
16 Morton, Richard. 1765 S.
17 Smith, Nathaniel. 1756 S.
18 Roberts & Briggs. 1860.
19 Butts, T. 1807.
20 Briggs, W. 1823.
21 Hutton, W. 1849.

MARKS USING SYMBOLS ONLY

22 Boulton, M & Co. 1784 S.
23 Fenton, Matthew & Co. 1760 S.
24 Watson, J & Son. 1830. Or Padley, Parkin & Co. 1849.
25 Smith, Sissons & Co. 1848.
26 Tudor & Leader. 1760 S.
27 Blagden, Hodgson & Co. 1821.
28 Walker, Knowles & Co. 1840.

22

23

24

25

26

27

28

3. Pewter

Pewter is an alloy of tin with lead, antimony or (notably in the case of fine old pewter) copper. Sometimes bismuth is added to harden the alloy. The proportions of the various metals in the alloy vary greatly, but generally speaking, the more tin, the better the pewter. Britannia metal is a close relative of pewter, and is of high quality, consisting mostly of tin with a small amount of antimony and copper.

Pewter-making began in the Middle Ages, when pewter plates replaced wooden ones, and remained popular into the 19th century, by which time china wares had taken over. A vast amount of domestic pewter ware was produced in Britain, including spoons, flatware, teapots, candlesticks and tankards (for domestic or tavern use), as well as church pewter. Yet, because of its low perceived value and the fact that it was often damaged in daily use, much old pewter has been lost.

As regards design, pewter ware in Britain has generally imitated silverware.

A large quantity of reproduction pewter has been made since the 1920s. Some of this, notably Liberty's Art Nouveau 'Tudric' range, is now quite collectable in its own right. However, most collectors prefer antique pewter, which is characterized by its glowing patina and its higher standards of finish as compared with reproduction pieces. It is the marks to be found on antique pewter which are covered here.

Standards of pewter

The Pewterers' Company regulated the quality of the alloy, in much the same way as the Goldsmiths' Company assayed silver and gold. The three principal types of pewter are, in ascending order of quality:

- Ley pewter: 80% tin, 20% lead
- Trifle pewter: 82% or 83% tin, 17% or 18% antimony
- Plate pewter: 86% tin, 7% antimony, 3.5% copper, 3.5% bismuth

Quality marks

Ley and trifle pewter did not carry any marks of quality. Plate pewter was marked with a letter 'X' (denoting extraordinary ware), sometimes with a crown above it (**1**), or else it was stamped with the words 'hard metal' or 'superfine hard metal' (**2**). A rose and crown stamp (**3**) also indicated fine quality pewter. At first this mark was for export ware only, although by the 18th century it had become more generally used. From the late 17th century, the word 'London' was added to the rose and crown, but it was often used by provincial pewterers also, and so is no guarantee of provenance.

1

2

3

Touch marks

By far the most important marks on pewter are the 'touch marks' or 'touches'. These identify the maker, and take their name from official 'touch plates' on which they were stamped when being registered at Pewterers' Hall. The earliest touch plates dated from the beginning of the 15th century but were lost in the Great Fire of London in 1666. The practice of registering marks on the touch plates began again two years later and continued until 1824.

The marks do not appear on the touch plates in chronological order, having been punched in any empty space in a haphazard fashion. Five copper touch plates survive at the Pewterers' Company, but the corresponding register of makers has been lost, making individual identification impossible in many cases.

A maker's touch mark often consisted simply of his initials or name, but could also incorporate elaborate designs, sometimes with a play on words based on the man's name. Dates also occasionally form part of the mark, but they indicate the year when the touch was registered rather than the year the piece was made.

The size of the touch marks varies according to the size of the item on which they appear, but as a very general rule, early marks tend to be smaller than later ones.

Other marks

Good early pewter often bears elaborate ownership marks in a raised form, rather like a wax seal. Triads (a triangular formation) of letters stamped on the rim of a pewter plate are generally held to give the initials of the couple who owned it.

Small marks are also found on pewter in imitation of silver hallmarks, and usually consist of four shields (**1**). The symbols in the shields generally imitate genuine silver marks quite closely – for instance, the figure of Britannia, the lion passant and the leopard's head – presumably with the purpose of persuading the buyer that the item concerned contained real silver.

After 1826, tankards and measures used in taverns had to carry capacity marks. These were of local design until 1877, after which they were validated by an excise mark consisting of a crown over the monarch's initials and a code number, denoting the area in which inspection of capacity had been carried out (**2**).

1

2

SAMPLE TOUCH MARKS

The touch marks shown on pages 156–159 are a small selection of examples where identification of the maker is possible. They are taken from Touch Plates I and IV at Pewterers' Hall, and serve to illustrate the variety that exists among the hundreds of touch marks registered there. If the touch mark you are seeking is not included, you should consult one of the specialist reference works on pewter marks in your local library. Note that 'master', 'warden', 'steward' and 'yeoman' were ranks and appointments within the guild structure of the Pewterers' Company.

1
R L
2
3
4
WA
5
T F
6
WILLIAM BURTON
7
R H
56
8
C
9
IOHN BULL
10
P P
1668
11
S
A
12
S
73

SAMPLE MARKS FROM TOUCH PLATE I

1 'RL' in an oval with a comet between the letters. Robert Lucas, who became a steward of the Pewterers' Company in 1651 and master in 1667.

2 'NK' in a beaded circle with a hand grasping a rose. Thought to be Nicholas Kelk, master in 1665, 1681 and 1686.

3 'SI' in a small beaded circle with a lamb and flag. Probably Samuel Jackson, working in the late 17th C.

4 'WA' in a small circle. Possibly William Austin or William Ayliffe, both working in the late 17th C.

5 'TF' in a beaded oval with a fountain. This is a pun on the maker's name, Thomas Fontaine or Fountain, who took up his livery in 1670.

6 'William Burton' in a beaded circle with a hand holding a sceptre. He was a warden in 1675 and 1680, and master in 1685.

7 'RH' in a beaded circle with a locust, three stars and the date [16]56. Ralph Hulls, warden in 1671 and 1677, master in 1682.

8 'C' in a beaded circle with a crown and cockerel. Another play on a name – Humphrey Cock, who took up his livery in 1679.

9 'John Bull' with a bull's head and two stars in a beaded circle. Late 17th C.

10 'PP' in a circle with a beacon and the date 1668. This could be the mark of Peter Parke or Peter Priest.

11 'SA' in a beaded circle with a lion rampant. Thought to be Sam Atley, who took his livery in 1667.

12 'SQ' in a beaded heart with an arrow and a key with the date [16]73. Thought to be Sam Quissenborough.

1
HENRY
MAXTED
2
JOHN
KENRICK
3
PHILIP
4
RC
5
I·PERRY
6
JOHN
7
JONATHAN
LEACH
8
THOMAS
GIFFIN
9
AJENNER
10
APPLETON
11
C·SWIFT
12
&
WOOD · HILL

SAMPLE MARKS FROM TOUCH PLATE IV

1 'Henry Maxted' with pillars and the sun shining on a rose. Yeoman 1731.
2 'Iohn Kenrick' with a stork between two pillars. Yeoman 1737, warden 1754.
3 'Philip Roberts' with a lion rampant and a crescent. Yeoman 1738.
4 'RC' in a beaded circle with a lamb holding a crook. Thought to be a play on the name Robert Crooke, yeoman 1738.
5 'I Perry' with a female figure between pillars. Yeoman 1743, warden 1773.
6 'Iohn Hartwell' with a saltire and four castles. Yeoman 1736.
7 'Ionathan Leach' with a quartered shield of arms showing a rose, a sprig of laurel and a lamb and flag. The fourth quarter is illegible. Yeoman 1732.
8 'Thomas Giffin' with a dagger piercing a heart and a ducal coronet, all between pillars. Yeoman 1759.
9 'A Jenner' in a plain rectangle. Thought to be Anthony Jenner, yeoman 1754.
10 'Jno Appleton' with a still and a worm. Yeoman 1768, warden 1799, master 1800.
11 'C Swift' in an indented square with a thistle and a rose (the badge of Queen Anne). Yeoman 1770.
12 'Wood & Hill' with two sheep in a shield. Thought to be Thomas Wood (yeoman 1792) and Roger Hill (yeoman 1791).

Note: 'I' was often used for 'J'. 'Ino' and 'Jno' stand for 'John'.

4. Pottery and porcelain

Unlike the strictly regulated hallmarks which appear on precious metals – and which give today's collector a foolproof means of identification – the marks that appear on pottery and porcelain are a far from reliable guide as to provenance.

Marks may be blurred and impossible to identify. A particular mark – say, an anchor – can indicate a wide variety of periods, factories and countries, and a true attribution can be given only by looking at the weight, colour, shape and pattern of the piece itself. The size and colour of the mark, as well as the way it was made, also have a bearing on its identification. Often marks have been used which imitated those of famous factories – for example there were endless copies of the Meissen crossed swords. Marks have also been added fraudulently at later dates.

If a piece of pottery bears no mark at all, it does not mean the piece is necessarily of an early date, because much pottery from every period bears no mark at all. Confusion may also result from the fact that a mark may refer to a factory, to a potter or painter who worked there, or to a past owner of the piece. Dates, too, are not to be taken at face value, because they rarely give the date of actual manufacture. When incorporated into a mark, a date commonly indicates the year when the factory was established, or when a particular design was introduced. However, the design registration marks which were applied from 1842 do give reliable dates for British wares thereafter. There were also a few factories which employed their own reliable dating systems, notably Sèvres, Derby, Minton and Wedgwood.

Pottery and porcelain are best understood by looking and touching, and the more you see and handle the various wares, the more of a feel you will get for them. Once you are more confident in your knowledge of the wares themselves, marks can be used as a very useful back-up. Nevertheless, approaching marks with a good deal of healthy suspicion is always to be recommended!

Pottery types

Pottery is made simply of clay, but many additions have been made to the clay mix to give added strength, and decorative glazes have been applied to enhance appearance. The following types are among the most common and important:

- *Creamware*: earthenware with a cream-coloured glaze, giving something of the impression of porcelain.
- *Delft*: Earthenware with a tin glaze, made in the 17th and 18th centuries.
- *Faïence*: Tin-glazed earthenware.
- *Majolica*: Decorative tin-glazed earthenware first made in 15th century Italy and copied in the 19th century.
- *Stoneware:* A strong non-porous ware made from adding sand or flint to the clay.
- *Ironstone*: Patented by Charles James Mason in 1813, using slag from iron furnaces to strengthen the wares.

Porcelain types

Porcelain was first made in China from the vital ingredients of kaolin (China clay) mixed with petuntse (China rock). It is recognized by its strength, its musical note when struck, and its translucent delicacy. From the moment porcelain was first imported in the 15th century, it was a huge success in Europe and there were many attempts made to reproduce it in the West. The ingredients for the hard paste porcelain of the Chinese original were eventually found at Meissen in what is now Germany, and porcelain production began there in the early 18th century. The process was then imitated throughout Europe.

Other experiments to imitate porcelain produced soft-paste porcelain, which has a less hard, glittery glaze than hard-paste porcelain, as well as less strength.

METHODS OF APPLYING MARKS

The way in which a mark is made can help in attributing it to a particular factory (as can its colour). Where relevant, this has been noted in the pages which follow. There are four main methods:

- *Incising*: This is one of the earliest and simplest methods, whereby a mark is scratched into the clay before it is fired.
- *Impressing: A* stamp is used to press a mark into the unfired clay.
- *Underglaze painting or transfer-printing*: Until 1850, this appeared only in blue, after which other colours were used. As the name suggests, the mark was made before the final glaze was applied over it.

• *Overglaze marks*: These may be painted, transfer-printed or stencilled onto finished wares. This method is a particularly easy one for forgers to imitate.

A thumbnail guide to establishing dates

- A printed mark signifies post-1800 manufacture
- Marks which include the royal arms appeared only after 1810
- Marks including the name of a pattern are also post-1810, and often much later
- The diamond registration mark indicates the period 1842–83 (see page 164)
- 'Limited' or 'Ltd' denotes 1860 onwards
- 'Trade mark' signifes 1862 onwards
- The practice of using 'Royal' followed by the manufacturer's name began in the mid 19th century
- 'Rd No' (Registered Number) was introduced in 1884
- The word 'England' was used from 1891 and 'Made in England' from early in the 20th century

REGISTERED DESIGN MARKS

The system of Registered Designs was devised in 1839 to protect the design of industrial products in much the same way that the patent laws protect inventions. There were two early layouts of Registration Marks, one in use from 1842 to 1867, the other from 1868 to 1883.

Mark layout 1842–67

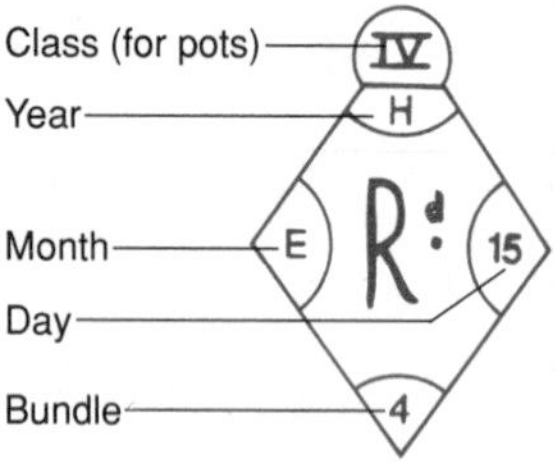
Class (for pots)
IV
Year
H
Month
E
Rd
15
Day
Bundle
4

Year codes 1842-67	
A 1845	N 1864
B 1858	O 1862
C 1844	P 1851
D 1852	Q 1866
E 1855	R 1861
F 1847	S 1849
G 1863	T 1867
H 1843	U 1848
I 1846	V 1850
J 1854	W 1865
K 1857	X 1842
L 1856	Y 1853
M 1859	Z 1860

Mark layout 1868–83

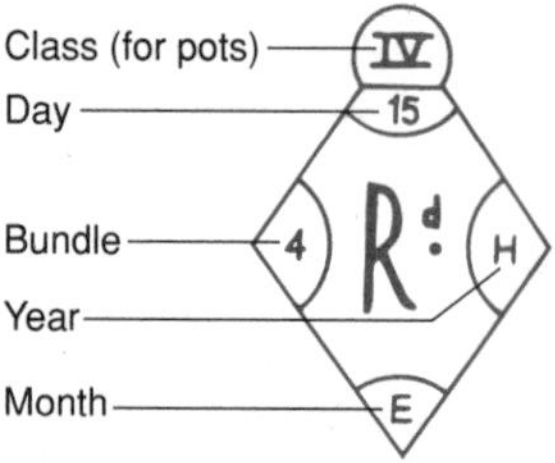
Class (for pots)
IV
Day
15
Bundle
4
Rd
H
Year
Month
E

Year codes 1868-83	
A 1871	K 1883
C 1870	L 1882
D 1878	P 1877
E 1881	S 1875
F 1873	U 1874
H 1869	V 1876
I 1872	X 1868
J 1880	Y 1879

Month codes 1842-83

The same system of code letters was used to indicate the month of registration on both types of design mark layout shown opposite.

A	December	E	May	K	November
B	October	G	February	M	June
C/O	January	H	April	R	August
D	September	I	July	W	March

REGISTRATION NUMBERS

From 1884, the complex diamond-shaped registration mark was replaced by a simple registration numbering system. The abbreviation 'Rd No' (for Registered Number) often appeared before the number. The system remains in use today. The dates of numbers used in the early years are given in the table below.

Rd No	Year	Rd No	Year
1	1884	291241	1897
19754	1885	311658	1898
40480	1886	331707	1899
64520	1887	351202	1900
90483	1888	368154	1901
116648	1889	385088	1902
141273	1890	402913	1903
163767	1891	425017	1904
185713	1892	447548	1905
205240	1893	471486	1906
224720	1894	493487	1907
246975	1895	518415	1908
268392	1896	534963	1909

1

2

3

4

5

6

7

8

9

10

11 Aaron Wood.

12 ADAMS

13 AMERICAN POTTERY Co JERSEY CITY N J

14 Apiello

15 AVALON

A

1 Paris, France. Painted red/gold. c1795.
2 Bow, London, England. Red. c1765.
3 Sèvres, France. Mark and date letter for 1753. Date letters ran alphabetically until 1793 (AA from 1778) appearing inside or alongside the 'crossed Ls' in blue (or later red) enamel.
4 Sèvres, France, 1778.
5 Nymphenberg, Germany. Impressed or incised. c1745.
6 Arras, France. Soft-paste porcelain. 1770–90.
7 'De Ster' (The Star), artist A Kiell. Delft, Holland. c1763.
8 Helene Wolfsohn, decorator. Meissen, Germany. c1860.
9 Meissen, Germany. Painted underglaze blue. c1725.
10 Thomas Allen (painter). Wedgwood. 1875–1905.
11 Burslem, Staffordshire, England. Impressed. c1750.
12 Adams & Co, Tunstall, England. From c1790.
13 New Jersey, USA. Printed. Mid 19th C.
14 Capo-di-Monte, Italy. Incised. c1760.
15 Cartwright Bros, East Liverpool, Ohio, USA. 1880–1900.

1 B

2 BARR FLIGHT & BARR.
Royal Porcelain Works.
WORCESTER.
London-House.
No. 1 Coventry Street.

3

4 +
B

5 B

6

7 B&G

8 •B•H•

9 BL

10

11 B.S.&T.

12 BELPER POTTERY
DENBY

14 Booth

13 6 Lompot

15 Bristoll

B

1 Flight & Barr, Worcester, England. Scratched in clay. 1793–1800. The most common Worcester marks are crescents, the letter W and copies of Chinese and Meissen marks.
2 Worcester. Printed. 1807–13. Later Worcester wares carry the full name.
3 Lille, France. Faïence. 1720–88.
4 Bristol, England. Painted. c1773.
5 Sèvres, France. 1754.
6 Bristol, England. 1773.
7 Bing & Grondahl, Copenhagen, Denmark. 1853.
8 Knoller, Bayreuth, Germany. Faïence. c1730.
9 Limbach, Germany. Porcelain. Late 18th C.
10 Niderviller, France. 1744–80.
11 Barker, Sutton & Till, Burslem, Staffordshire, England. 1830-50.
12 Belper Pottery, Derbyshire, England. Stoneware. 1812.
13 'De Vergulde Bloompot' (The Golden Flowerpot), Delft, Holland. c1693.
14 Enoch Booth, Tunstall, Staffordshire, England. Impressed. c1750.
15 Bristol, England. Porcelain. c1750.

1
2
3
4
5
6
7
8
9
10
11
12
13
14
15
CD
CGW
CM
Chelsea
1745
16
Chamberlain's

C

1 Nantes, France. c1780.
2-6 Caughley, England. Variations of the Caughley mark, printed or painted in underglaze blue between 1772–95.
7 Bayreuth, Germany. Painted. 1744.
8 Castel-Durante, Italy. c1570.
9 'De Ster' (The Star), C D Berg, Delft, Holland. c1720.
10 Coalport, Coalbrookdale, England. Hard-paste porcelain. Painted blue. c1825–50.
11 Limoges, France. Hard-paste porcelain. c1783.
12 Coalport, Coalbrookdale, England. Hard paste porcelain. Painted blue. Early 19th C.
13 Leeds, England. c1760.
14 St Cloud, France. Faïence/porcelain. c1711.
15 Chelsea, London, England. Soft-paste porcelain c1745.
16 Worcester, England. Red. 1788–1808.

1
2
3
4
5
6
7
8
DL
9
10
DP.
11
12
Derby
13
D & Co
FRANCE.
14
D. D. & Co.
CASTLEFORD
15

D

1 Davenport, England. Impressed. 1793–1882.
2 Derby, England. 1770–84.
3 Caughley, England. Hard-paste porcelain. Painted blue. c1750.
4 Derby, England. Soft-paste porcelain. Red. c1756.
5 John Donaldson (painter), Worcester, England. Porcelain. c1770.
6 Derby (Chelsea), England. c1782.
7 Coalport, Coalbrookdale, England. Painted blue. c1825–50.
8 William Littler, potter, Longton Hall, Staffordshire, England. 1750–60.
9 Louis Dorez, Nord, France. c1735.
10 Proskau, Silesia, Germany. Faïence. 1770–83.
11 'De Paauw' (The Peacock), Delft, Holland. Faïence. c1700.
12 Derby, England. Incised. c1750.
13 Limoges, France. c1875.
14 Castleford, England. Pottery. Impressed. c1790.
15 J van Duyn, 'De Porceleyne Schootel' (The Porcelain Dish), Delft, Holland. Faïence. Painted blue. c1764.

1 E

2 E

3 E
1779

4 EB

5 Ef

6 E. I. B.

7 E.L
1754

8 E
M+B
J760

9 E.Borne
1689

10 ENGLAND

11 ENOCH BOOTH
1757

12 Enoch Wood

13 E. NORTON
BENNINGTON
VT.

14

15
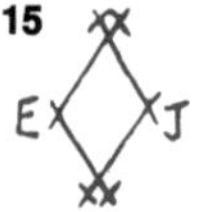

E

1 Elton Pottery, Somerset, England. 1880–90.
2 St Petersburg, Russia. 1762–96.
3 Derby, England. 1779.
4 Paris, France. c1800.
5 Moustiers, France. Faïence. 18th C.
6 Hanley, England. Impressed. 18th C.
7 Bow, London, England. c1754.
8 Michael Edkins and his wife, Bristol, England. Blue. c1760.
9 Henri Borne, Nevers, France. c1689.
10 From 1891, the word 'England' appeared on English wares.
11 Tunstall, Staffordshire, England. c1757.
12 Burslem, England. Impressed, moulded or incised. 1784–90.
13 Bennington, Vermont, USA. Impressed. c1882.
14 Ernst Teichert, Meissen, Germany. Late 19th C.
15 E Jacquemin, Fontainebleu, France. 1862–66.

1

2

3

4

5

6

7

F B

8

FBB

9

10

F
Z

11

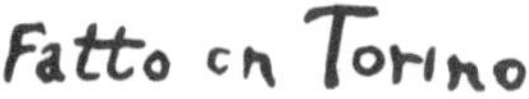
Fatto cn Torino

12

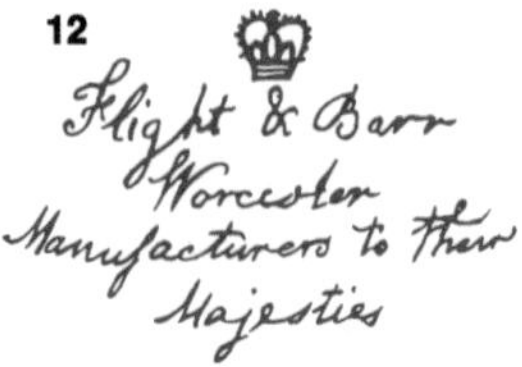
Flight & Barr
Worcester
Manufacturers to their
Majesties

F

1 Rouen, France. Faïence. c1644.
2–3 Variations of mark of Furstenberg, Germany. 1760–70.
4 Jacob Fortling, Copenhagen, Denmark. Faïence. 1755–62.
5–6 Variations of mark of Bow, London. 1750–59.
7 Francois Boussemart, Lille, France. c1750.
8 Flight, Barr & Barr, Worcester. 1813–40.
9 Rouen, France. 1673–96.
10 Buen Retiro, Madrid, Spain. Soft-paste porcelain. c1759.
11 Turin, Italy. Faïence. 16th C.
12 Flight & Barr, Worcester, England. 1792–1807.
13–14 Variations of Worcester Flight marks. 1782–91.
15 Bordeaux, France. 1781–87.
16 Fulper Bros, Flemington, New Jersey, USA. Impressed. 19th C.

13

14

15

16
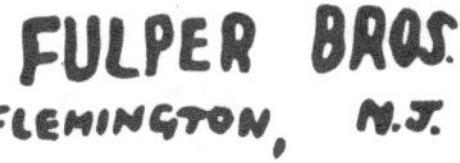

1

2

3

4
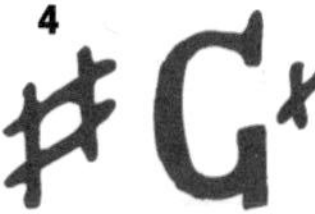

5

6

7

8

9

10

11

12

13

G

1 Bow, London, England. Porcelain. 1744–60.
2 Bow, London, England. Porcelain. 1750–70.
3–4 Tavernes, France. Faïence. 1760–80.
5 Faenza, Italy. 15th C. The town of Faenza gave its name to faïence.
6 Buen Retiro, Madrid, Spain. Soft-paste porcelain. 1759–1808.
7 Gotha, Germany. Hard-paste porcelain. Painted blue. 1775–1800.
8 Gotha, Germany. Painted blue. 1805–30.
9 Unger, Schneider, Thuringia, Germany. 1861–87.
10 Nicolas Gardin, Rouen, France. c1760.
11 Limoges, France. 1842–98.
12 Swansea, Wales. 1765–1870.
13 Emile Galle, Nancy, France. Early 20th C.
14 Guy Green, printer, Liverpool, England. 1756–99.
15 Limoges, France. c1773.
16 Alcora, Spain. Faïence/ porcelain. c1750.

14

GREEN

15

GR et Cie

16

GROS

1

2

3

4

5

6

7

8

9

10

11

12

13

HP
1636

14

HARTLEY, GREEN & CO.

H

1–2 Hannong, Faubourg St Lazare, Paris, France. c1773.
3 Strasburg, Germany. Faïence/porcelain. c1750.
4 Nevers, France. Faïence. 17th C.
5 D Hofdick, 'De Ster' (The Star), Delft, Holland. Faïence. c1705.
6 Antoine de la Hubaudiere, Quimper, France. c1782.
7 Faincerie de la Grande Maison, Quimper, France. c1898–1902.
8 Delft, Holland. Faïence. 17th C.
9–10 Hannon & Laborde, Vincennes, France. c1765.
11 Prague, Germany. Porcelain. 1810–35.
12 Humphrey Palmer (potter), Hanley, England. c1760.
13 Winterthur, Switzerland. Faïence. 17th C.
14 Leeds, England. Pottery. c1750.
15 Hugo Booth, Stoke-on-Trent, England. c1785.
16 Henry Roudeburth, Montgomery, Pennsylvania, USA. Early 19th C.

15

16

1 I

2 +I+ +

3 I·B

4 iB *

5 I.C.

6 I.E.1697

7 I.W

8 IE:W:1699: WROT:HAM

9 I.Smith

10 IRESON

11 I. & G. RIDGWAY

12 IRONSTONE B & M

13 I. SEYMOUR TROY

14 I. B. FARRAR & SONS

I

1 Bow, London, England. Painted red or blue. 1744–59.
2 St Cloud, France. Faïence/porcelain. 1678–1766.
3 Bristol, England. Painted blue or gold. 1770–81.
4 'De Ster' (The Star), Delft, Holland. Faïence. Painted blue. c1764.
5 John Crolius, New York, USA. Impressed. c1790.
6–8 Variations on mark from Wrotham, England. Slipware. 17th or 18th C.
9 Joseph Smith, Wrightstown, Pennsylvania, USA. c1775.
10 Nathaniel Ireson (potter), Wincanton, England. Tin-glazed earthenware. 1740–50.
11 Job Ridgway, Hanley, Staffordshire, England. Earthenware. 1802–8.
12 Bagshaw & Meir, Burslem, Staffordshire, England. Earthenware. Printed or impressed. 1802–8.
13 Israel Seymour, Troy, New York, USA. Impressed. c1825.
14 Isaac Farrar, Fairfax, Vermont, USA. c1800.
15 J Dale(potter), Burslem, Staffordshire, England. Late 18th C–early 19th C.
16 Lisbon, Portugal. c1773.

15

16

1

2

3

4

5

6
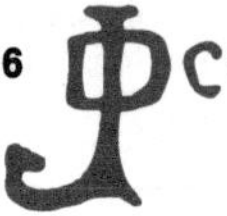

7

8

9

10

11

12

13

14
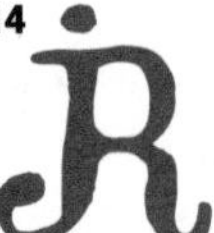

15

J

1 Longton Hall, Newcastle, England. Porcelain/stoneware. 1750–60.
2 Ilmenau, Thuringia, Germany. Faïence/porcelain. c1777.
3 Ilmenau, Thuringia, Germany. 1900–40.
4 Copenhagen, Denmark. 1750–60.
5 Aprey, France. Faïence. c1750.
6 J Dimmock & Co, Hanley, Staffordshire, England. Late 19th C.
7 G Jones & Sons, Stoke-on-Trent, England. Late 19th C–early 20th C.
8 James Hadley & Sons, Worcester, England. 1896–1903.
9 Bell Works, Shelton, England. Pottery. Printed. 1770–1854.
10 St Cloud, France. Soft-paste porcelain. 1678–1766.
11 Jacob Petit (potter), Fontainebleu, France. Hard-paste porcelain. Painted blue. c1800.
12 Jean Pouyat (potter), Limoges, France. Painted red. 1842.
13 John Remney, New York, USA. Stoneware. c1775.
14 Joseph Robert (potter), Marseilles, France. Porcelain. 1754–93.
15 Ashby Potters Guild, Burton-on-Trent, England. Pottery. Early 20th C.

1 K

2 K

3 K

4 K

5 K. H.
P. A

6 K.H.C.W

7 K.P.M

8 K.P.M.

9 Keeling Toft & Co.

10 K & G
LUNEVILLE

11 KIEBZ
13
II

12 Kishere

13 KLUM

K

1 Klosterle, Bohemia, Germany. Porcelain, lead-glazed earthenware. 1794–1803.
2 Jan Kuylich, Delft, Holland. Faïence. Painted blue. 17th C.
3 Jan Kuylich the younger, Delft, Holland. Faïence. Painted blue. Registered 1680.
4 Kiel, Germany. Faïence. c1770.
5 Meissen, Germany. Hard-paste porcelain 1720–60.
6 Königliche Hof Conditorei, Meissen, Germany. Hard-paste porcelain. Painted blue. 1720–60.
7 Königliche Porzellan Manufaktr, Meissen, Germany. Hard-paste porcelain. Underglaze blue. c1723.
8 Krister, Germany. 19th C.
9 Keeling (potter), Hanley, Staffordshire, England. Impressed. 1806–24.
10 Keller & Guerin (owners), Luneville, France. Faïence. 1778.
11 Kiev, Russia. Porcelain. 1798–1850. Stoneware. 1800–11.
12 Joseph Kishere (potter), Mortlake, England.
13 Klum, Germany. Porcelain. 1800–50.
14 Smith-Phillips China Co, East Liverpool, Ohio, USA. Late 19th C.
15 Knowles, Taylor & Knowles, East Liverpool, Ohio, USA. Established 1854.

14

KOSMO

15

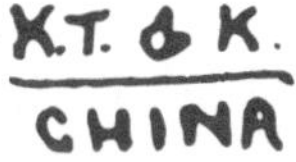
K.T. & K.
CHINA

1
2
3
4
5
6
7
8
9
10
LO
11
LEEDS POTTERY
12
LEEDS · POTTERY
LEEDS · POTTERY

L

1–3 Jean-Joseph Lassia (proprietor), Paris, France. Porcelain. 1774–84.
4 Lille, France. Hard-paste porcelain. Late 18th C.
5 Tours, France. Faïence. c1756.
6 Valenciennes, Nord, France. Faïence. 1735–80.
7 Limbach, Thuringia, Germany. Hard-paste porcelain. Painted red. c1772.
8 Buen Retiro, Spain. Soft-paste porcelain. 1759–66.
9 Valenciennes, Nord, France. Faïence, hard-paste porcelain. c1785.
10 St Cloud, France. Faïence, porcelain. 1678–1766.
11–13 Leeds, England. Creamware. Late 18th C.
14–16 Limbach, Thuringia, Germany. Late 18th C.

13

14

15

16

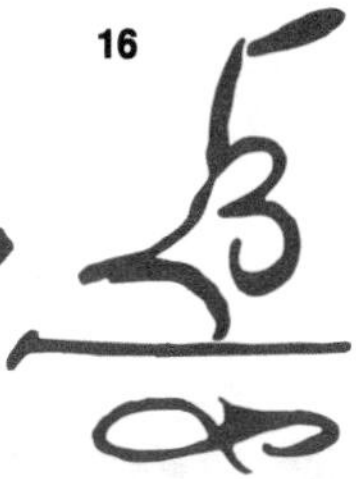

13

MASON'S PATENT
IRONSTONE CHINA

14

M

1–2 Rouen, France. 1720–30.
3–4 Minton, Stoke-on-Trent, England. Underglaze blue. 1800–30.
5 Longton Hall, Newcastle, Staffordshire, England. 1750–60.
6–7 Pierre Roussencq (founder), Marans, France. Faïence. Late 18th C.
8 Moreau Ainé, Limoges, France. Late 19th C.
9 Arnoldi, Germany. Early 19th C.
10 Mennecy, France. Porcelain. 1734–73.
11 Herculaneum, Liverpool, England. 1833–41.
12 Schmidt Brothers, Germany. Late 18th C.
13 Mason, Fenton, England. Faïence. Printed. 1813.
14 Meissner Porzellan Manufaktur, Dresden, Germany. Hard-paste porcelain. c1723.
15 Minton & Boyle, Stoke-on-Trent, England. Impressed. 1836–41.
16 Mayer & Newbold (potters), Hanley, England. Early 19th C.

15

M&B
FELSPAR PORCELAIN

16

M. & N.

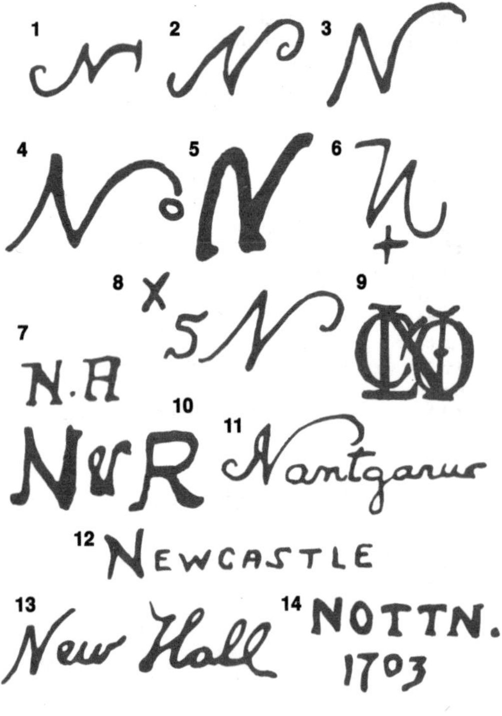
1
2
3
4
5
6
7
N.A
8
5N
9
10
N&R
11
Nantgarw
12
NEWCASTLE
13
New Hall
14
NOTTN.
1703

N

1 Niderviller, France. Faïence. Mid to late 18th C.
2 Derby, England. Incised blue or red. c1770.
3 New Hall, Shelton, England. Painted red. 1782–1810.
4 New Hall, Shelton, England. Painted black. 1782–1810.
5 Nove, Venice, Italy. 1800–25.
6 Limbach, Germany. Porcelain. Late 18th C.
7 Wrotham, England. 17th C.
8 Bristol, England. Pottery, porcelain. Overglaze blue or gold. 18th C.
9 Urbino, Italy. Pottery. 16th C.
10 Christian Nonne & Roesch (owners), Ilmenau, Thuringia, Germany. Porcelain. c1786.
11 Nantgarw, Wales. Hard-paste porcelain. Painted red. c1811.
12 Newcastle-upon-Tyne, England. Pottery. Impressed. c1800.
13 New Hall, Shelton, England. Painted red. Late 18th C.
14 Nottingham, England. Pottery. c1705.
15 Niderviller, France. Faïence. Mid to late 18th C.
16 Bassano, Italy. Soft-paste porcelain. c1760.

15

16

1 O

2 G

3 OB

4 OP

5 OS

6 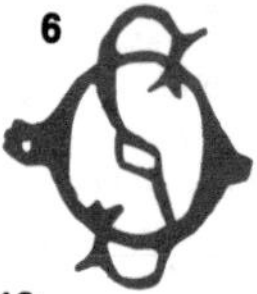

7 O.V.

8 ·OY.

10 OLDFIELD & CO.

9 O. & B.

11 OLIVER
A PARIS

12 OPAQUE CHINA

13 Opaque China
B.B. & I.

14 ORIENTAL
STONE
J. & G. ALCOCK

15 Orleans

16 OWENS
UTOPIAN

O

1 Bow, London, England. Porcelain. c1750.
2 St Petersburg, Russia. Porcelain. c1760.
3 Mennecy-Villeroy, France. Porcelain, faïence. Mid 18th C.
4 Mennecy-Villeroy, France. Porcelain, faïence. Painted blue. c1773.
5 George Oswald (painter and potter), Ansbach, Bavaria, Germany. 1692–1733.
6 Oscar Schlegelmilch, Thuringia, Germany. Late 19th C.
7 Ohio Valley China Co, Wheeling, West Virginia, USA. c1890.
8 Olerys & Laugier (managers), Moustiers, France. Hard- and soft-paste porcelain. c1739.
9 Ott & Brewer, Trenton, New Jersey, USA. c1880.
10 Brampton, England. Brownware. c1825.
11 Olivier (potter), Paris, France. Faïence. Late 18th C.
12 Cambrian, Wales. Earthenware. c1807.
13 Baker, Bevans & Irwin, Swansea, Wales. c1830.
14 J & G Alcock, Cobridge, England. Mid to late 19th C.
15 Duke of Orleans (patron), Loiret, France. Mid 18th C.
16 J B Owens Pottery Co, Zanesville, Ohio, USA c1890.

1
2
3
4
5
6
7
8
9
10
11
PA
12
13
14
15
P. P. Coy. L.
Stone China
16
poupre
a japonne

P

1–2 Seth Pennington (potter), Liverpool, England. Painted gold or colour. Late 18th C.
3–4 James & John Pennington (potters & painters), Liverpool, England. Painted gold or colour. Mid 18th C.
5–6 Pinxton, Derbyshire, England. Soft-paste porcelain. 1796–1813.
7 St Cloud, France. Faïence, porcelain. Mid 18th C.
8 Nymphenberg, Germany. Porcelain. Impressed or incised. Mid 18th C.
9 Philippe-Auguste Petit (potter), Lille, France. Painted colour. c1778.
10 Pigory (owner), Chantilly, France. Soft-paste porcelain. Early 19th C.
11 Rouen, France. Faïence. Painted colour. 16th or 17th C.
12 Moustiers, France. Faïence. Mid 18th C.
13 Paul Hannong (proprietor), Strasburg, France. Underglaze blue. 1740–60.
14 Paris, France. 1786–1793.
15 Plymouth, Pottery Co, Plymouth, England. c1850.
16 Moulins, France. Faïence. c1730.

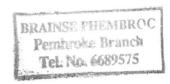

1
R
2
R
3
R
4
R
5
R
6
R
7
R
8
R
9
RB
10
R
11
12
RAINFORTH & CO.
13
Rockingham
14
R Hancock fecit

R

1 Louis-François Roubiliac (sculptor), Chelsea, London. Impressed. c1738.
2 Bristol, England. Porcelain. c1750.
3 Marseilles, France. Porcelain. 1773–93.
4 Bow, London, England. Porcelain. 1750–60.
5 Joseph Gaspard Robert (potter), Marseilles, France. Faïence. 1754–93.
6–7 Rauenstein, Thuringia, Germany. Porcelain. 1783.
8 Rouen, France. 16th–17th C.
9 Bow, London, England. Porcelain. 1750–60.
10 Sèvres, France. Hard- and soft-paste porcelain. Painted blue, gold. 1793–1804.
11 Meissen, Germany. Hard-paste porcelain. Underglaze blue c1730.
12 Rainforth (potter), Leeds, England. Late 18th or early 19th C.
13 Rockingham, Swinton, Yorkshire, England. Late 18th or early 19th C.
14 Worcester, England. Hard-paste porcelain. 1756–1774. 'Made by R Hancock'.
15 William Reid (potter), Liverpool, England. Porcelain. Impressed. 1755–59.
16 Ralph Toft (potter), Wrotham, England. Slipware. c1677.

15

16

1 

2 

3 

4 

5 

6 

7 

8 

9 SX

10 Sx

11 Sx

12 S.A. & CO.

13 Sadler

14 **SALOPIAN**

15 SPODE.

16

SPODE & COPELAND

S

1 St Petersburg, Russia. Hard-paste porcelain. Painted blue. c1744.
2–3 Caughley, England. Hard-paste porcelain Painted blue. 1755–99.
4 Rouen, France. Faïence. c1760.
5 St Cloud, France. Faïence, porcelain. 1678–1766.
6 Eisenach, Germany. Mid to late 19th C.
7 Schlaggenwald, Bohemia, Germany. Porcelain. 1793–1866.
8 Joseph Flower (painter), Bristol, England. Delft. 1739–51.
9–10 Jacques Chapelle (potter), Penthieve factory, Sceaux, Seine, France. Soft-paste porcelain. 1749–63. Later 'Sceaux' painted in blue.
11 Caughley, England. Porcelain. 1750–1814.
12 Smith, Ambrose & Co, Burslem, Staffordshire, England. c1800.
13 John Sadler (engraver), Liverpool, England. Pottery and hard- paste porcelain. Printed. 1756–70.
14 Caughley, England. Porcelain. Impressed. 1750–1814. Caughley factory taken over in 1799 by Coalport.
15 Spode. Stoke-on-Trent, England. Porcelain. Impressed. Painted red, blue, black or gold. c1770.
16 Spode & Copeland, Stoke-on-Trent, England. 1770–97.

1

2

3

4

5

6

7

8

9

Jannova

10

T. FELL & CO.

11

T. FLETCHER & CO.

12
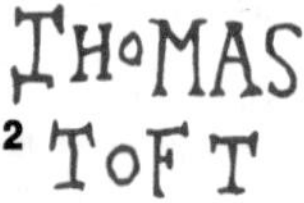
THOMAS
TOFT

13

Théodore Haviland
Limoges
FRANCE

T

1–3 Thomas Frye (manager), Bow, London. Porcelain. 1744–59.
4 Tebo (modeller), Bristol, England. Porcelain. 1770–75.
5 Tite Ristori, Nevers, France. Pottery. c1850.
6 Torquay, Devon, England. Terracotta. 1875–1909.
7 Nevers, France. Faïence. 18th C.
8 T Vickers, Lionville, Pennsylvania, USA. c1805.
9 Tannowa, Bohemia, Germany. Faïence, porcelain. 1813–80.
10 Thomas Fell (potter), Newcastle, England. c1817.
11 T Fletcher (owner), Shelton, England. 18th C.
12 Thomas Toft (potter), Burslem, England. Slipware. c1670.
13 Theodore Haviland, Limoges, France. c1920.
14 Theodore Haviland, New York, USA. Printed green or black. c1936.
15 Warne & Letts, South Amboy, New Jersey, USA. c1806.
16 Theodore Deck, Paris, France. Faïence. c1859.

14

15

16

1
U. & C.
2
3
4
V&B
M
5
CHELSEA
6
7
8
9
10
Ve M
& C
11
Vena
12
VILLEROY & BOCH
13
Velazqz
14
VC

U/V

1 J Uffrecht, Haldensleben, Germany. Late 19th C.
2 Sarreguemines, France. Faïence, porcelain, c1770.
3 Nathaniel Hewelcke (potter), Venice, Italy. Porcelain. Incised. 1757–63.
4 Villeroy & Boch, Mettlach, Saar, Germany. 1890–1910.
5 Charles Vyse, Chelsea, London. Early 20th C.
6–7 Veuve Perrin (potter), Marseilles, France. Faïence. Painted black. c1790.
8 Jan van der Kloot, Delft, Holland. Faïence. Painted blue. c1765.
9 Baron Jean-Louis Beyerle, Niderviller, France. Faïence. 1754–70.
10 Rue Thiroux factory, Paris, France. Hard-paste porcelain. c1775.
11 Venice, Italy. Hard-paste porcelain. c1700.
12 Villeroy & Bosch (potters), Mettlach, Germany. Faïence. c1842.
13 Buen Retiro, Spain. Hard-paste porcelain. 1759–1808.
14 Alcora, Spain. Porcelain, faïence. Mid 18th C.
15 Varages, France. Faïence. 18th C.
16 Vinovo, Italy. Porcelain. Underglaze blue or incised. c1775.

15

16

1

2

3

4

5

6

7

8

9

10

11

12

13

W

1 Plymouth, England. Hard-paste porcelain painted blue. c1768.
2 Plymouth, England. Painted red, blue, gold. c1768.
3 Thomas Wolfe (potter), Stoke-on-Trent, England. Impressed. 18th–19th C.
4–8 Variations of the Worcester mark. Hard-paste porcelain, 1775–83.
9 Rouen, France. Faïence. c1720.
10–11 Wegeley (founder), Berlin, Germany. Porcelain. 1751–60.
12 Bristol, England. c1853.
13 Chelsea, London, England. Porcelain. 1745–84.
14–15 Variations of the Worcester mark. Late 18th C.
16 Absolon (enameller), Yarmouth, England. c1800.

14

15

16

1 Walton

2 W. & B.

3 Wedgwood

4 WEDGWOOD

5 WEDGWOOD & CO

6 Wedgwood & Co.
Ferrybridge

7 WEDGWOOD
ENGLAND

8 WEDGWOOD

9 WINCANTON

10 

11 

12 

13 

14 

W, X, Y, Z

1 John Walton (potter), Burslem, England. Earthenware. 18th–19th C.
2 Wedgwood & Bentley, Staffordshire, England. Earthenware. 1769–80.
3 Wedgwood, Etruria, England. Pottery. Impressed. c1771.
4 Wedgwood, Etruria, England. Impressed on pottery, 1771. Printed red, blue, gold on porcelain, 1812–6.
5–6 Ralph Wedgwood, Ferrybridge, England. Stoneware. Impressed. 1796–1800.
7 Wedgwood. Pottery. After 1891.
8 Wedgwood. Pottery. Impressed. After 1780.
9 Wincanton, Bristol, England. Earthenware. 17th C.
10–11 Vaux (or Bordeaux), France. Hard-paste porcelain. Late 18th C.
12 'De Griekse A' (The Greek A), Delft, Holland. c1674.
13–15 Zurich, Switzerland. Pottery, Hard-paste porcelain. Painted blue. Late 18th C.
16 Worcester. 1775–85.

15

16

1

2

3

4

5

6

7

8

9

10

11

12

13

ANCHORS

1–4 Chelsea, London, England. Porcelain. Underglaze blue, gold. 1750–69.

5 Chelsea, London, England. Soft-paste porcelain Painted gold or red. c1745.

6 Chelsea, London, England. Soft-paste porcelain. Underglaze blue or red, blue, purple. 1749–56.

7 Derby-Chelsea, England. Porcelain. Painted blue, lilac or gold. c1770.

8 Derby, England. Porcelain. c1745.

9 Bow, London, England. Hard-paste porcelain. Painted red or blue. c1744.

10 Bow, London, England. Soft-paste porcelain. Painted red or brown. c1760–80.

11–12 Bow, London, England. Soft-paste porcelain. Painted red, brown or blue. c1760–80.

13 Bow, London, England. Porcelain. 1745–70.

14 Liverpool, England. Cream earthenware. 1793–1841.

15 Sceaux factory, Seine, France. Porcelain, faïence. c1775.

16 Thomas Fell (potter), Newcastle, England. Impressed. 18th–19th C.

14

15

16

1

2

3

4

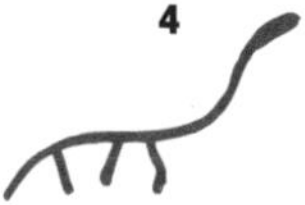

5

6

GRIFFIN

7

8

9

Baguley
Rockingham Works.

10

BELLEEK

11

TRADE
MARK
WEDGWOOD & Co.

12

ANIMALS, FISHES AND INSECTS

1 Furstenberg, Germany. Porcelain. 18th C.
2 Hesse Cassel, Germany. Hard-paste porcelain. Painted blue. c1763.
3 Oiron, France. 16th C.
4 'De Klauw' (The Claw), Delft, Holland. Mid 18th C.
5 Edgem Malkin, Burslem, England. Late 19th C.
6 Williamson, Longton, England. Early 20th C.
7 Frankenthal, Bavaria, Germany. Hard-paste porcelain. Painted blue. c1754.
8 Amsterdam, Holland. Hard-paste porcelain. Painted blue. c1772.
9 Rockingham, Swinton, England. Hard-paste porcelain. Painted red. c1824.
10 Belleek, Ireland. c1860.
11 Ralph Wedgwood, Burslem, England. 1796–1800.
12 Lille, France. Hard-paste porcelain. Stencilled and painted red. c1784.
13–14 Nyon, Switzerland. Hard-paste porcelain. Underglaze blue. c1780.
15 Seville, Spain. Glazed pottery. 19th C.

13

14

15

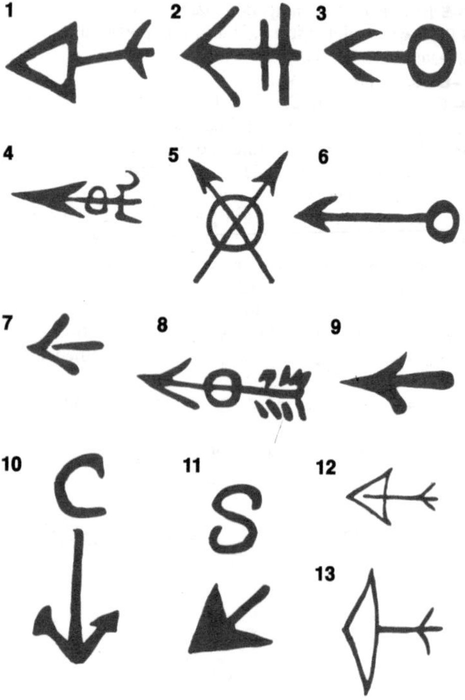
1
2
3
4
5
6
7
8
9
10
C
11
S
12
13

ARROWS

1–5 Bow, London, England. Porcelain. c1750.
6 Plymouth, England. Hard-paste porcelain. Painted blue. 1768–70.
7–8 Leeds, England. Pottery. Impressed. c1774.
9–11 Caughley, England. Hard-paste porcelain. Painted blue. Mid–late 18th C.
12 Derby, England. Porcelain. c1830.
13 Derby, England. Porcelain. 1745–1848.
14 Robert Allen (painter), Lowestoft, England. Porcelain. 1757–80.
15 W Absolon (enameller), Yarmouth, England. Porcelain, earthenware. Impressed. Early 19th C.
16 Rue de la Roquette factory, Paris, France. Hard-paste porcelain. Painted blue. c1774.
17 La Courtille factory, Paris, France. Hard-paste factory. Underglaze blue, incised. c1771.

14

15

16

17

1
A
2
3
4
5
6
ENGLAND
7
BM&T
8
9
10
11
S
5
12
AAPC
UNGAREN
13
WH Goss
14

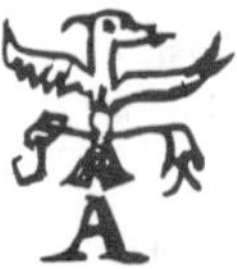

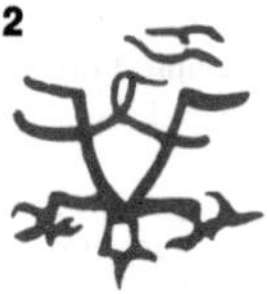

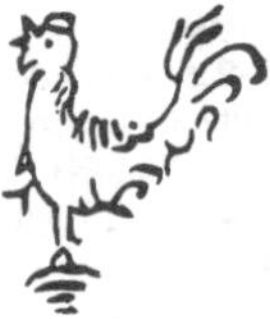

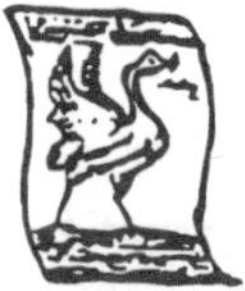

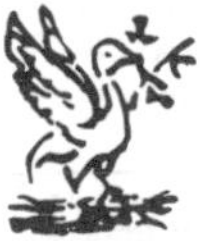

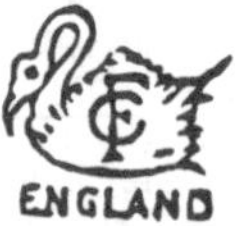

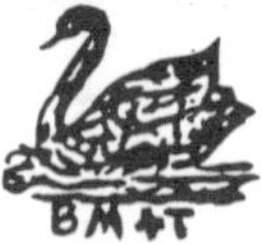

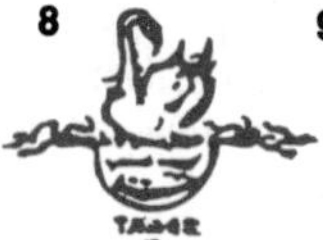

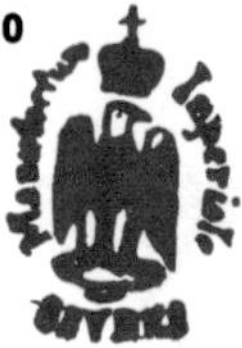

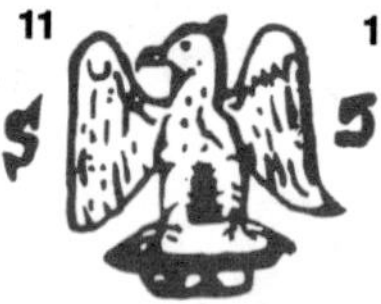

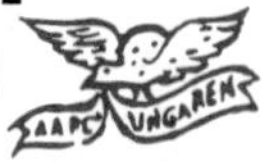

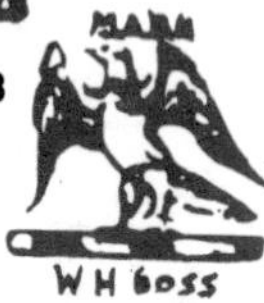

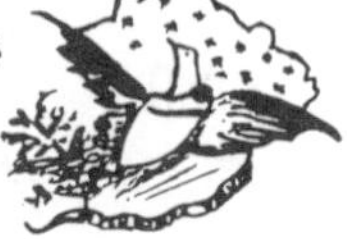

BIRDS

1–2 Ansbach, Bavaria, Germany. Hard-paste porcelain. Painted blue. c1765.

3 J V Kerckof (artist), Amsterdam, Holland. 1755–70.

4–5 Herculaneum factory, Liverpool, England. c1833.

6 Charles Ford, Burslem, England. 19th C.

7 Boulton, Machin & Tennant, Tunstall, England. Late 19th C.

8 T Rathbone, Tunstall, England. Early 20th C.

9 Limoges, France. 1842–98.

10 Sèvres, France. Hard-paste porcelain. Painted red. c1810.

11 Sèvres, France. Hard-paste porcelain. c1852.

12 Homer Laughlin China Co, East Liverpool, Ohio USA. Late 18th C.

13 W H Goss, Stoke-on-Trent, England. Late 19th C.

14 T Mayer, Stoke-on-Trent, England. c1829.

15 Florence, Italy. Faïence. Late 19th C.

16 Hanks & Fish, Swan Hill Pottery, South Amboy, New Jersey, USA. c1849.

15

16

1
2
3
4
5
6
7
8
9
10
11
E WOOD & SON BURSLEM.
SEMI CHINA
WARRANTED
12
F N
J
13
ORLEANS
M·B

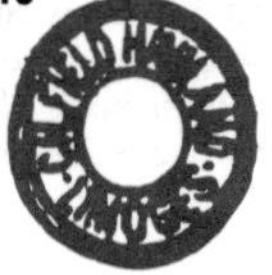

CIRCLES

1–2 Faenza, Italy. Faïence. 16th–17th C.
3 Spode, Stoke-on-Trent, England. Impressed. Late 18th C.
4 Hochst, Germany. Hard-paste porcelain. Painted blue, red, gold. 1750–65.
5–6 Worcester, England. Hard-paste porcelain. Underglaze blue. Late 18th C.
7 Bow, London, England. Soft-paste porcelain. Late 18th C.
8 Ken & Binns, Worcester, England. Porcelain. 1852–62.
9 Wedgwood & Bentley, Etruria, England. 1769–80.
10 Charles Field Haviland Co, Limoges, France. c1882.
11 Enoch Wood & Sons, Burslem, England. c1790.
12 Ilmenau, Germany. Porcelain. 19th C.
13 Orleans, France. Hard-paste porcelain. c1800.
14 Urbino, Italy. Pottery. 16th C.
15 Cologne, Germany. Pottery. 17th C.
16 Minton, Stoke-on-Trent, England. Hard-paste porcelain. Printed. 1800.

14

15

16

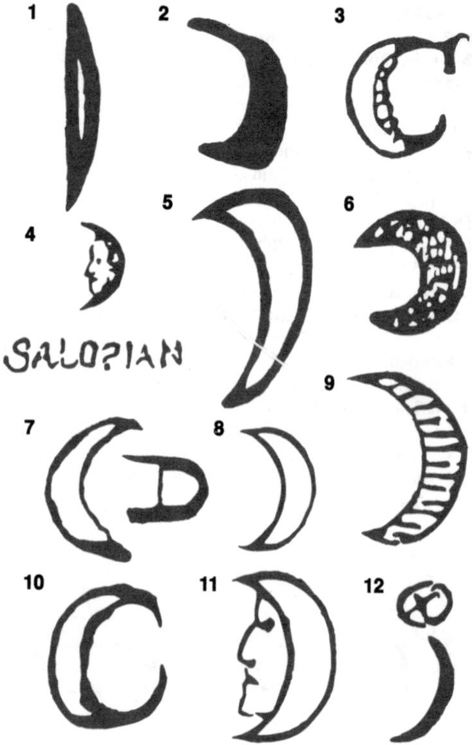
1
2
3
4
5
6
SALOPIAN
7
8
9
10
11
12

CRESCENTS

1–2 Bow, London, England. Porcelain. c1750–75.
3–7 Caughley, England. Painted blue. c1775–99.
8–11 Worcester, England. Hard-paste porcelain. c1751–1800.
12 Nymphenburg, Germany. Porcelain. Impressed or incised. Mid to late 18th C.
13 Pinxton, England. Soft-paste porcelain. 1796–1801.
14 Turkey. Porcelain. c1850.
15 Munden, Germany. Faïence.18th C.
16 Faenza, Italy. Faïence. 16th C.

13

14

15

16

1

2

3

4

5

6

7

8

9

10
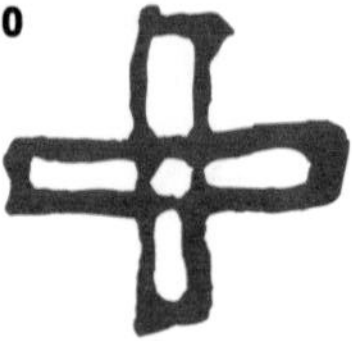

11

12

13

14

LINES AND CROSSES

1 St Petersburg, Russia. Hard-paste porcelain. Painted blue. Late 18th C.
2 Royal Copenhagen Factory, Copenhagen, Denmark. 1830–45.
3 Royal Copenhagen Factory, Copenhagen, Denmark. c1775.
4 Varages, France. Faïence. c1770.
5–6 Bristol, England. Porcelain. Painted colour. c1770.
7 Leeds, England. Painted colour. c1770.
8 Chelsea, London, England. Porcelain. 1745–84.
9 Nymphenburg, Germany. Porcelain. Impressed or incised. Late 18th C.
10 Bow, London, England. Mid 18th C.
11 Copenhagen, Denmark. c1770.
12–14 Bow, London, England. Mid 18th C.
15 Meissen, Germany. 19th C.
16 Longton Hall, Staffordshire, England. 1749–60.
17 Caughley, England. 1775–99.

15

16

17

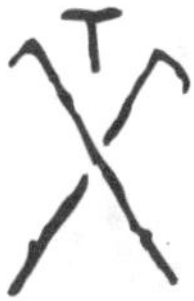

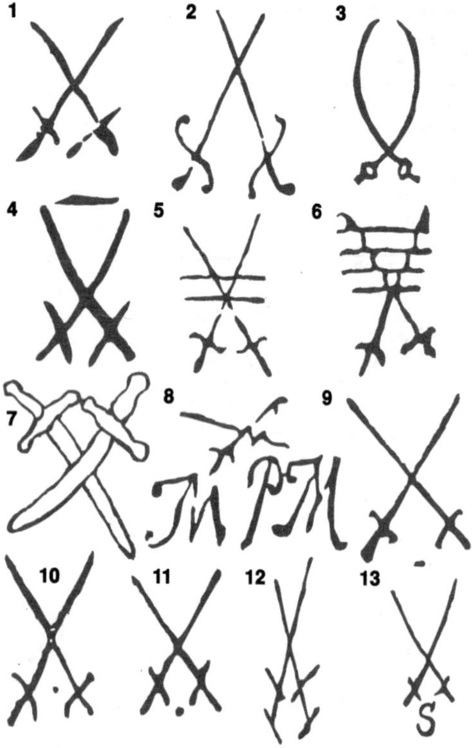
1
2
3
4
5
6
7
8
MPM
9
10
11
12
13
S

CROSSED SWORDS

1–8 Marks from the Meissen factory in Germany, all painted blue.
1 Early 18th C.
2–3 c1730.
4–6 Mid 18th C.
7–8 c1723.
9 Worcester, England. Mid 18th C.
10 Bristol, England. Porcelain. Painted blue, gold. Mid 18th C.
11 Derby, England. Mid 18th C.
12 Coalport, Coalbrookdale, England. Early 19th C.
13 Samson, Edme, Paris, France. Late 19th C.
14 Caughley, England. Painted blue. 1775–99.
15 Jacob Petit, Fontainebleu, France. 1830–40.
16–17 Bristol, England. Porcelain. Painted blue or gold. 1773–81.

14

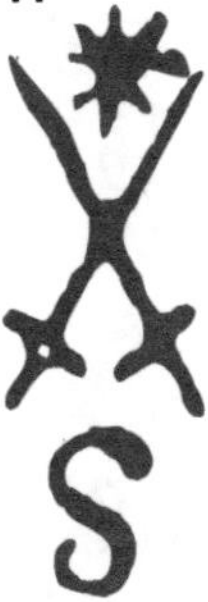

15

16

17

1
2
3
4
5
6
Flight
7
8
9
10
29
11
12
G
13

CROWNS

1 Derby, England. 1775–70.
2 Bloor, Derby, England. 1811–48.
3 Vincennes, France. Hard-paste porcelain. c1765.
4 Derby, England. Painted red or violet. c1780–4.
5 Belleek, Ireland. Late 19th C.
6 Worcester, England. c1813–40.
7 Derby, England. c1784–1815.
8 Royal Crown Derby, Derby, England. 1877–9.
9 Sèvres, France. 1773.
10 Sèvres, France. 1824–30.
11 Meissen, Germany. 1720–50.
12 Leeds, England. Earthenware. Mid 18th C.
13–14 St Petersburg, Russia. Porcelain. Painted colour. Late 18th C.
15 Herculaneum, Liverpool, England. Impressed or printed. 1800–41.
16 James Clews (potter), Cobridge, England. Earthenware. Blue printed. c1819–29.

14

15

16

1

2

3

4

5

6

7

8

9
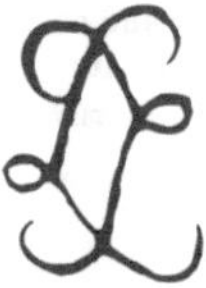

10

11
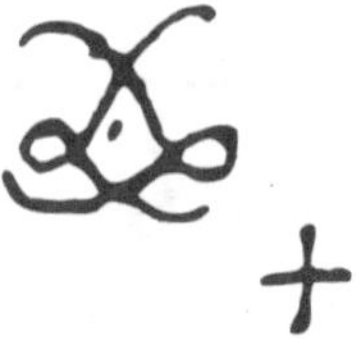

CURVES

1–5 Sèvres, France. Soft-paste porcelain. 1745–53.
6–8 Sèvres, France. Soft- and hard-paste porcelain. 1764–71.
9 Worcester, England. Mid 18th C.
10 Minton, Stoke-on-Trent, England. 18th C to 1831.
11 Coalport, Coalbrookdale. Porcelain. Early 19th C.
12–13 Buen Retiro, Madrid, Spain. 1759–1808.
14 Niderviller, France. Late 18th C.
15 Nuremburg, Germany. Early 18th C.
16 Nymphenburg, Germany. c1747.

12

13

14

15

16

1

2

3

4

5

6

7

8

9

10

11

FLEURS-DE-LYS

1 St Cloud, France. Soft-paste porcelain. Impressed. c1680–1766.
2 Rouen, France. Faïence. Painted colour. 16th C.
3 Bow, London, England. Soft-paste porcelain. Painted blue. c1730.
4–5 Marseilles, France. Faïence. Late 18th C.
6–8 Buen Retiro, Madrid, Spain. Soft-paste porcelain. 1759–1808.
9–10 Ginori, Italy. Painted blue. 1820–50.
11 Minton, Stoke-on-Trent, England. Painted green. After 1850.
12 Capo di Monte, Naples, Italy. 1730–40.
13 Orleans, France. 1753–1812.
14–15 Lowesby, England. Mid 19th C.

12

13

14

15

1

2

3

4

5

6

7

8

9

10

11

12

13

FLOWERS AND TREES

1–4 'De Roos' (The Rose), Delft, Holland. Late 17th C.
5 Longport, Staffordshire, England. c1825.
6 Rose & Co, Caughley, England. Hard-paste porcelain. Painted colour. 1799.
7 Coalport, Coalbrookdale, England. Early 19th C.
8 Volkstedt factory, Thuringia, Germany. Porcelain. Late 18th C.
9 Greuby Faïence Co, Boston, Mass., USA, c1900.
10 Imenau, Germany. Faïence, porcelain. Late 18th C.
11 Limbach, Thuringia, Germany. Porcelain. Late 18th C.
12–13 Grosbreitenbach, Germany. Hard-paste porcelain. Painted colour. Late 18th C.
14 Berlin, Germany. Hard-paste porcelain. Painted blue, green or gold. c1800. Often on damaged pieces.
15 Delft, Holland. Faïence. 18th C.
16 'De Ster' (The Star), Delft, Holland. Faïence. c1720.

14

15

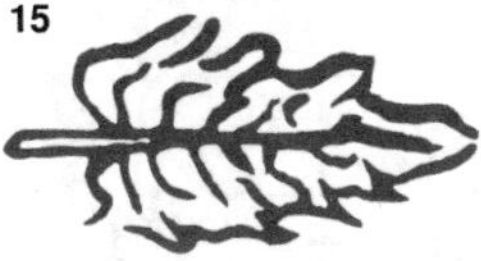

16

1

2

3

4

5

6

7

8

9

10

W.&.B.LTD

11

PORCELAINE OPAQUE
TRADE MARK
BRIDEWOOD & SON

12

ENOCH WOOD & SONS
BURSLEM.

13

ZELL

14

ANHERST JAPAN
No 62
STONE CHINA

SHIELDS

1–2 Royal Factory, Vienna, Austria. Hard-paste porcelain. Painted blue. 1750–80.
3–5 Royal Factory, Vienna, Austria. Incised. 1744–1820.
6 Nymphenburg, Germany. Porcelain. 1754–1862.
7–8 Nymphenburg, Germany. c1800.
9 Ansbach, Germany. Hard-paste porcelain. Painted blue. Mid to late 18th C.
10 Wood & Barker, Burslem, England. 19th C.
11 Bridgwood & Son, Longton, England. 19th C.
12 Enoch Wood & Sons, Burslem, England. 1818–46.
13 Zell, Germany. Glazed earthenware. After 1818.
14 Stoke-on-Trent, England. Porcelain. c1799.
15 Copeland & Garrett, Spode, Stoke-on-Trent, England. 1833–47.
16 Minton, Stoke-on-Trent, England. After 1868.

15

16

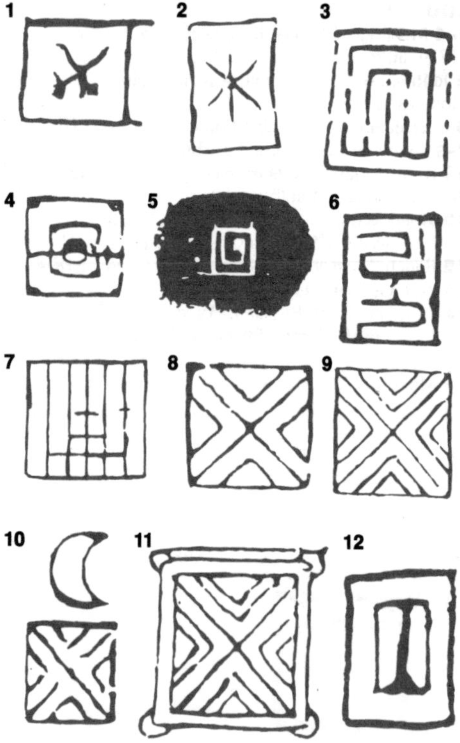
1
2
3
4
5
6
7
8
9
10
11
12

SQUARES

1–4 Meissen, Germany. Bottger red stoneware. c1710–20.
5 John & David Elers (potters), Newcastle, England. Stoneware. c1690–1710.
6 Chelsea, London, England. Porcelain. 1745–85.
7–11 Worcester, England. Porcelain. Late 18th C.
12 Derby, England. Painted blue. c1775.
13–14 Bow, London, England. Mid 18th C.
15 Mayer & Newbold, Longton, Staffordshire, England. Painted red. 19th C.
16 Baden, Germany. Mid 18th C.

13

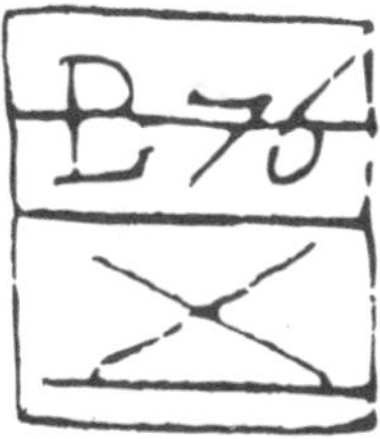

14

15

16

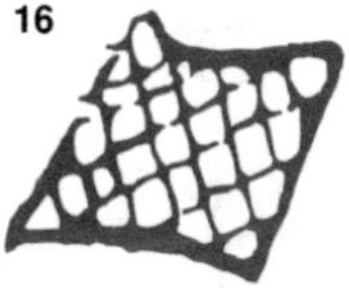

1

2

3

4

5

6

7

8

9

10

11

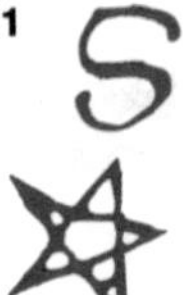

12

13

STARS AND SUNS

1 Isaac Farnsworth, Derby, England. 18th–19th C.
2/5/6 Ginori, Doccia, Italy. 1735–7.
3 Wallendorf, Thuringia, Germany. Porcelain. c1764.
4 'De Ster' (The Star), Delft, Holland. Faïence. c1690.
7 Caughley, England. Porcelain. c1750.
8 Nove, Italy. Faïence, porcelain. Painted gold. Mid 18th C.
9 Wedgwood, Etruria, England. Impressed. 1765–1850.
10 Nymphenburg, Germany. Hard-paste porcelain. Late 18th C.
11 Savona, Italy. 18th C.
12 Seville, Spain. 19th C.
13 Nevers, France. Faïence. 17th C.
14–15 St Cloud, France. Soft-paste porcelain. Painted blue. 1678–1766.
16 Robert Bloor, Derby, England. c1811–48.

14

15

16

1

2

3

4

5

6

7
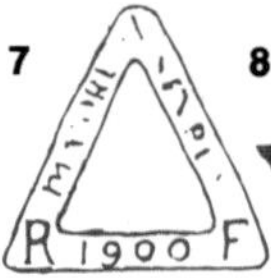
R 1900 F

8

H.43.

9

BURSLEM.

10

S
1900

11

TRADE
MARK

12

TRADE
MARK
C
T
M

13

TRIANGLES AND HEARTS

1–2 Chelsea, London, England. Soft-paste porcelain. Painted gold or red. c1745–50.
3–4 Bow, London, England. Incised. Painted blue. Mid 18th C.
5 Derby, England. Hard-paste porcelain. Impressed. Painted blue. Mid 18th C.
6 Bristol, England. Hard-paste porcelain. Impressed. c1763–73.
7 Sèvres, France. 1900–2. Mark tells year of decoration.
8 Meissen, Germany. Porcelain. Impressed. c1766–80.
9 Burslem, England. 19th C.
10 Sèvres, France. Hard-paste porcelain. Painted black. Soft-paste painted blue. c1900–11.
11 Hanley, England. 19th C.
12 Newcastle, England. 19th C.
13 Orleans, France. Hard and soft paste porcelain. Painted colour. c1753–1812.
14 Rue Popincourt factory, Paris, France. Porcelain. c1782–1835.
15 Richard Chaffers, Liverpool, England. c1740–65.
16 Bruges, Belgium. 18th C.

14

15

16

1

2

3

4

5

6

7

8

9

10

ORIENTAL COPIES

1–6 Worcester marks, 1751–83.
7 Caughley, England. c1772–99.
8 Burslem, England. Late 17th or early 18th C.
9–11 Meissen, Germany. Bottger ware. Early 18th C.
12 Samson 'the Imitator', Paris, France. Found on imitation Lowestoft (England). c1875.
13 Coalport, Coalbrookdale, England. Hard-paste porcelain c1828–50.
14 Delft, Holland. Faïence. Painted blue. c1800.
15 'De Romeyn' (The Roman), Delft, Holland. Faïence. c1671.

11

12

13

14

15

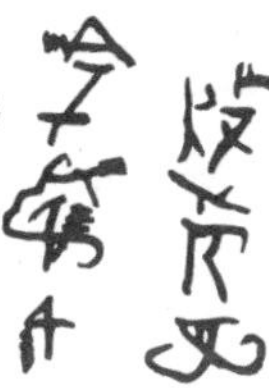

1
CAMPANIA
T & R BOOTE
ROYAL SEMI PORCELAIN
ENGLAND
2
PRIZE MEDAL
T & R. BOOTE.
3
Stevenson
4
5
R$
6
7
8
S
9
10
11
12
13
14
T&V
15
16
JB
17
18
Cambrian Pottery
19
COPELAND LATE SPODE
20
MEDINA
TG
21
OLD HALL
22
23
24

MISCELLANEOUS

1–2 T & R Boote, Burslem, England. Late 18th C.
3 Cobridge, Staffordshire, England. Painted blue. c1800.
4 Delft, Holland. Faïence.18th C.
5 'De Oude Moriaan's Hooft' (The Old Moor's Head), Delft, Holland. Faïence. c1680.
6 Royal Vienna Factory, Austria. c1850.
7 Derby, England. Hard-paste porcelain. Painted blue. 1745–1848.
8 Paris. Hard-paste porcelain. Painted gold. c1870.
9 Caughley, England. Porcelain. 1750–1814.
10 Clignancourt, France. Hard-paste porcelain. c1771–5.
11 Worcester, England. c1751–83.
12 Chantilly, France. Soft-paste porcelain. Painted blue or red. c1725–1800.
13 J & M P Bell & Co, Scotland. Late 19th C.
14 Limoges, France. Hard-paste porcelain. c1736–96.
15–16 Bellevue Pottery Co, Hull, England. Earthenware. c1825.
17 Savona, Italy. 17th C.
18 Cambrian factory, Swansea, Wales. Soft-paste porcelain. c1765.
19 W T Copeland & Sons, Spode, Stoke-on-Trent, England. Porcelain. c1847.
20 Burslem, England. c1795.
21 Old Hall Pottery, England. Earthenware. 19th C.
22 Tournay, Belgium. Soft-paste porcelain, late 18th C.
23 Clignancourt, France. Hard-paste. Painted blue, gold. c1771–98.
24 Savona, Italy. 18th C.

25

26

27

28

29

30

31

32

33

34

35

36

37

38

39

40

25–27 Bristol, England. Pottery, porcelain. Painted blue or gold. 18th C.
28 Nevers, France. Pottery. Painted colour. 16th C.
29–31 Plymouth, England. Hard-paste porcelain. Painted red, blue or gold. c1768.
32–34 Royal Factory, Berlin, Germany. Hard-paste porcelain. Painted blue. c1760.
35 Hanley, England. 19th C.
36 Nymphenburg, Germany. Porcelain. Impressed or incised. Late 18th C.
37 Caughley, England. Hard-paste porcelain. Painted blue. c1750.
38 Bow, London, England. Porcelain. c1750.
39 Bristol, England. Hard-paste porcelain. Painted colour. c1770.
40 Bristol, England. Hard-paste porcelain. Printed blue. c1800.
41 Job Ridgways (potter), Shelton, England. c1794.
42 Podmore, Walker & Co, Staffordshire, England. c1755.

41

42

5. Oriental porcelain

The marks that appear on Chinese and Japanese wares are quite different from their Western counterparts – and not merely in the matter of script. When European traders began importing Chinese porcelain in the 15th and 16th centuries, it was assumed that the marks indicated the names of the makers. British and European potters and factories accordingly followed suit, each maker displaying his own mark. In fact, Chinese marks do not refer to potters at all, but either indicate the emperor in whose reign a piece was made, or represent symbols of good omen or commendation.

False Marks

Identifying oriental porcelain by its marks alone is difficult and potentially risky. The marks often imitate those of earlier periods, either as a gesture of respect towards ancestors, or as simple forgery. The accurate identification of oriental ware requires above all a knowledge of period and factory styles – the marks can be regarded, at best, as a back-up.

CHINESE PORCELAIN

Porcelain was a Chinese discovery and its manufacture dates back to the 9th century AD, although other forms of pottery have been found in China dating from many centuries earlier. The great periods for Chinese porcelain are generally considered to be the reigns of the Ming and the Ch'ing Emperors, at the beginning of which porcelain became fashionable.

Reading Chinese marks

Chinese script reads in columns from right to left. Most marks consist of two columns of three characters each. To read them, go from top to bottom of the right-hand column, then top to bottom of the left.

The first two characters signify the word 'great' (ta) (**1**), followed by the name of the dynasty (**2**). The next two characters represent the reign-name – usually the Emperor's first and second names (**3**, **4**). The final two are 'period' (nien) (**5**) and 'make' (chih) (**6**).

(There was also a dating system based on a 60-year cycle, using two symbols, but these alternative marks were rarely applied and are difficult to interpret.)

In marks where there are only four characters, the dynasty is omitted. There is also an alternative form consisting of a square seal mark, written in an archaic script known as 'seal character'.

Example of a six-character mark

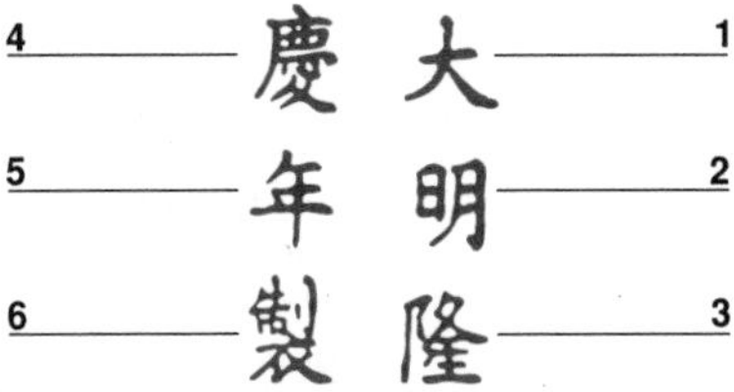

Ming dynasty
Lung Ch'ing (Longqing) 1567–72

Principal Chinese Dynasties

Dynasty	Dates
Shang Yin	1760–1120 BC
Chou	1120–249 BC
Ch'in	221–206 BC
Han	206 BC–AD 220
Six Dynasties	AD 220–589
T'ang	AD 618–906
Five Dynasties	AD 907–960
Sung	AD 960–1279
Yuan	AD 1279–1367
Ming	AD 1368–1644
Ch'ing	AD 1644–1916

Ming and Ch'ing (Qing) dynasties

These two dynasties are the most important as regards Chinese porcelain. The Ming dynasty was established in 1368 and consisted of 17 reigns, ending in 1644. Power then passed to the Ch'ing (Qing) dynasty, which consisted of 11 reigns and lasted until 1916.

Ming means 'bright' and Ch'ing (Qing) means 'pure'.

Ming dynasty reign marks

1 Hung-wu (Hongwu), 1368–98
2 Chien-wen, 1399–1402
3a Yung-lo (Yongle), 1403–24
3b (in archaic script)
4 Hung-hsi, 1425
5a Hsuan-te (Xuande), 1426–35
5b (in seal characters)
6 Cheng-t'ung, 1436–49
7 Ching-t'ai, 1450–57
8 T'ien-shun, 1457–64
9a Ch'eng-hua, 1465–87
9b (in seal characters)

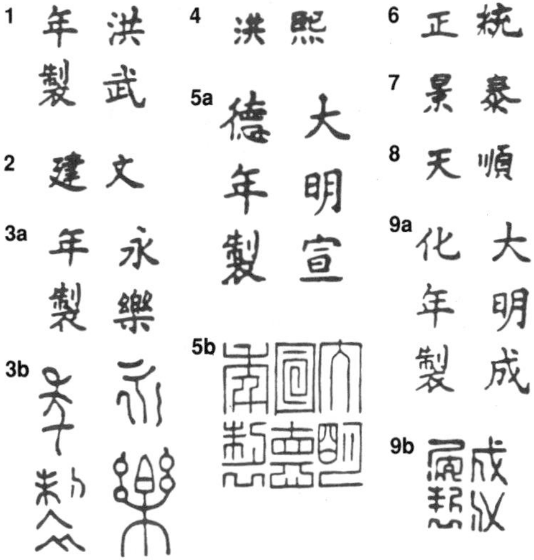

10 Hung-chih (Hongzhi), 1488–1505
11 Cheng-te (Zhengde), 1506–21
12 Chia-ching (Jiajing), 1522–66
13 Lung-ch'ing (Longqing), 1567–72
14 Wan-li (Wanli), 1573–1619
15 T'ai-ch'ang (1620)
16 Tien-ch'i (Tianqi), 1621–27
17 Ch'ung-cheng (Chongzhen), 1628–43

10 大明弘治年製

11 大明正德年製

12 大明嘉靖年製

13 大明隆慶年製

14 大明萬曆年製

15 泰昌

16 大明天啟年製

17 崇禎年製

Ch'ing (Qing) dynasty

1a Shun-chih (Shunzhi), 1644–61
1b (in seal characters)
2 K'ang-hsi (Kangxi), 1662–1722
3a Yung-cheng (Yongzheng), 1723–35
3b (in seal characters)
4a Ch'ien-lung (Qianlong), 1736–95
4b (in seal characters)
5a Chia-ch'ing (Jiaqing), 1796–1821
5b (in seal characters)

1a 大清順治年製

3a 大清雍正年製

4b 大清乾隆年製

1b 大清順治年製

3b 大清雍正年製

5a 嘉慶年製

2 大清康熙年製

4a 大清乾隆年製

5b 大清嘉慶年製

6 Tao-kung (Daoguang), 1821–50
7a Hsien-feng (Xianfeng), 1851–61
7b (in seal characters)
8a T'ung-chih (Tongzhi), 1862–73
8b (in seal characters)
9a Kuang-hsu (Guangxu), 1874–1908
9b (in seal characters)
10 Hsuan-t'ung (Xuantong), 1909–12
11 Hung-hsien (Hongxian), 1916

6

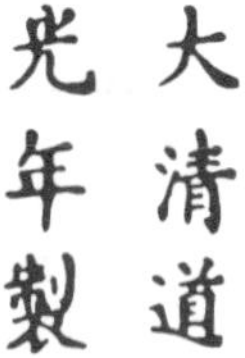

8a

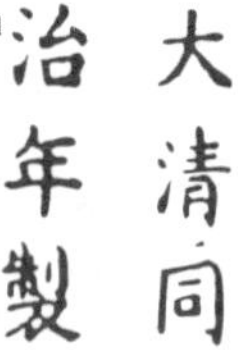

9b

10

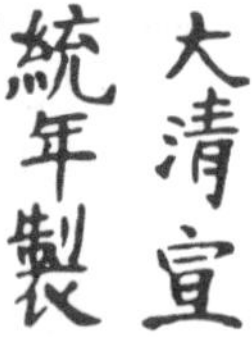

7a

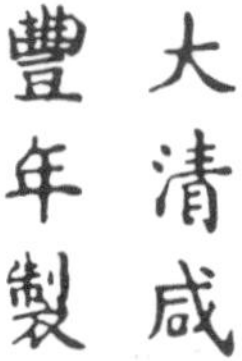

8b

9a

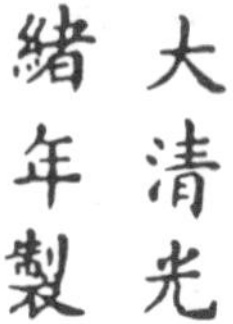

11

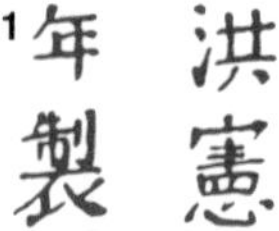

7b

JAPANESE PORCELAIN

Porcelain was first made in Japan in the early 17th century, beginning with the early Arita wares. Decoration, especially for export to Europe, often followed the Chinese style. However, there are a number of distinctive Japanese styles, among them Imari with its popular vivid red, blue and gilded vases and dishes; Kakiemon, with its beautiful enamel decoration; and Nabeshima, which used delicate underglaze blue and enamel decoration.

Japanese marks

Japanese marks are even more unreliable than Chinese ones. They include not only copies of Chinese marks, but names of potters, patrons and places. However, much of the best Japanese porcelain bears no marks at all, and very few marks appear before the end of the 18th century.

A few common examples of Japanese marks have been included here for reference.

'Raku' seal

'Kenzan' signature

'Banko' seal

Two forms of 'fuku' (meaning happiness)

'Kutani'

Impressed signature of 'Ninsei'

COLLINS GEM
BABIES' names
a
?
z
a mine of information

COLLINS GEM
BEER
a mine of information

COLLINS GEM
BIRDS
a mine of information

COLLINS GEM
CALORIE
Counter
a mine of information
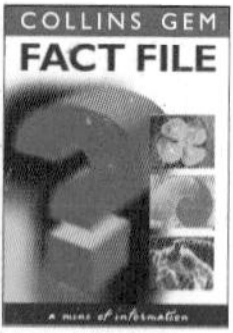
COLLINS GEM
FACT FILE
a mine of information

COLLINS GEM
FENG SHUI
a mine of information

COLLINS GEM
FLAGS
a mine of information

COLLINS GEM
Healthy
EATING
a mine of information

COLLINS GEM
QUOTATIONS
a mine of information

COLLINS GEM
SAS
Self-Defence
a mine of information

COLLINS GEM
SAS
Survival Guide
a mine of information

COLLINS GEM
SEASHORE
a mine of information

COLLINS GEM
TREES
a mine of information

COLLINS GEM
Understanding
DREAMS
a mine of information

COLLINS GEM
WILD
flowers
a mine of information

COLLINS GEM
WINE
Dictionary